Vix, the Lockdown Fox

Marion Veal

Dedication

For my parents, June and Sid who taught me to love animals and the natural world,

and for my husband Brian and our wonderful life of adventures together.

ACKNOWLEDGMENTS

No book is ever the work of the author alone, no matter how much they may wish it.

Thanks to my brother, David, who, despite rolling his eyes at me, came to understand that our What's App chats would be cut short by the arrival of a fox.

Special thanks go to Sue Skinner, the first person to read the whole book, for spotting typographical errors and suggesting improvements.

To Mew and Jem for their constant love and support.

To the members of the Self Isolating Bird Club, later the Friends of the Self-Isolating Bird Club for their kindness, encouragement and support through one of the most difficult years of my life and for helping me appreciate there was a life beyond grief.

To all the new friends I have made through Vix.

Keep up to date with my wildlife world at *marionveal.com* and Marion Veal Author and Wildlife Enthusiast on Facebook.

Introduction

What do you see when you look into the eyes of an animal? Are you afraid? Or do you find a connection with another sentient being traced back through millennia to a long forgotten common ancestor? Do you sense each other's fear or curiosity? Do you acknowledge the constant struggle for existence? Do you understand each other? I felt I did with Vix.

When our eyes first met, she was suffering. Her coat was thin, her tail a long thread and her eyes downcast. She was wary and fearful. Her ears twitched, listening for any sign of danger. Her eyes darted this way and that as she scanned the surroundings. And then they fell upon me. She froze. Humans usually mean danger to foxes; something to be avoided. If she had a genetic memory, it might warn her of being pursued by hounds and red-coated predators on horseback; of cowering in a hole as barking dogs clawed at the ground or a race for survival as men with guns chased her across fields and through woods. Or perhaps her family memories involved large noisy machines on wheels with glaring lights and blaring horns that left her relatives battered and bruised, limping or dead in the gutter.

Whatever thoughts went through Vix's mind the moment our eyes met, they did not seem to frighten her too much because she stayed in my garden. She watched me, assessed me, and found someone she could trust.

What I saw was a fellow living being with eyes that revealed a sadness I knew all too well, Vix was a woman alone facing an uncertain future. We were kindred spirits. I did not know how to help myself through the grief I felt but, I was certain there would be something I could do to help this fox. I had seen too much death. I did not want to watch another living being die.

And so, our story begins.

If you just want to read about Vix, then I suggest you skip ahead to 'Before Lockdown' because I am going to witter on a bit at first about other animals that have meant a lot to me and helped me along life's metaphorical highway. It is a bit like sitting through the support act while you wait for the reason you paid for an expensive concert ticket to walk out on stage. Not that Mew and Jem are the support act. To me they are the main event but even they would agree that we would not be here if it were not for Vix. However, if it were not for them, Vix would have been just another fox in my garden. If it were not for the other extraordinary animals I have encountered in my life, I would never have felt confident enough to help Vix, and Mew and Jem have saved me from the darkest of days so please give them a moment too.

I apologise if the photographs are not of the highest quality but as you will understand they were not taken with publication in mind and are not something I can go back and reshoot. However, I believe this book would be diminished if we could not see the beautiful animals I talk about.

So, grab a cuppa and a dippy biscuit. Maybe a chocolate digestive or a malted milk, or, if you are feeling extravagant, a piece of lemon drizzle cake. Sit yourself down in your favourite chair, turn off your phone and I will begin.

Prologue

My husband once told me, 'You collect strays'. At the time he was referring to himself, having needed scooping-up after some mishap, usually involving him not knowing where his car was in a car park or having forgotten something I later produced from my bag, having picked it up on the way out of the house because I knew he would need it but not take with him. He also said it with a mind to the fact that I scoop up animals and other people too.

When my husband and I were out together he would often return from a trip to get a drink or collect something from the car and find me comforting a lost child or giving a bewildered youngster, directions to somewhere.

"How do you do it?" he would ask, with a shake of his head, once the child was safely on their way.

"I think it's some sort of internal magnet," I would reply, equally bewildered by the skill I appear to have. "Children just seem to gravitate towards me."

Even on a recent visit to the British Wildlife Centre I encountered a small girl who, despite the presence of her grandparents walked straight up to me and said, "Can I show you the owls?"

"Yes," I replied. We looked at a long-eared owl who, she informed me, was grumpy because people kept taking his photograph.

"Come and see the barn owl," she instructed.

"We're going to see the barn owls," I informed her grandparents and we all dutifully followed the little girl, in pink wellies, as she and I chatted about the different owls and which one was her favourite.

I could imagine Brian, shaking his head and smiling as he asked, "How do you do it?"

"I don't know."

After a while Brian was no longer surprised by whatever waif or stray, I would be found with next.

I am a teacher, so keeping an eye out for children and what they are up to is second nature to me, so it is not surprising that I spot one in need of help. However, I think it is also about eye contact and the awareness of others. Some people go through life ignorant of the world around them. I seem acutely aware of people in close proximity, and perhaps, due to a lack of self-esteem, I have always been aware of others and if they are looking at me. I also have excellent peripheral vision. I scour the environment around me; possibly from some instinctive sense of self-preservation but for whatever reason I notice things. When on a safari holiday in Kenya, many years ago, I spotted puffs of dust coming from a small hole in the ground. We stopped the land cruiser and peered down to see the two enormous incisors of a rodent in its burrow. It may have been a naked mole rat; not one of the Big Five, but it was exciting all the same. I will spot the burrowing rodent or the lost child; I will notice their body language and I will make eye contact. It is at that point, somehow sensing that I am not a danger, they approach.

I also have a particularly good memory for how I have felt in certain situations. That first day at school, first day in a new job, being overwhelmed by the task ahead and, I know what it is like to feel alone or scared. Knowing that, I can empathise with others and I will do my best to put them at their ease or at least make the situation less fearful. I have been told that I have a nurturing nature and am a 'carer'. I have been that in all senses of the word. I hate to see someone suffer be it a person or animal and if I can do something to make them feel better, I will. My husband also said I was 'soft' and he meant it as a compliment. I am soft. I do care. I make no apologies for that. I think the world could use a few more soft people.

But caring and doing something about it are two different things. We may care about the victims of a disaster, but do we all send donations, campaign for injustice or speak up for others? And what has any of this got to do with a fox? I suppose I am trying to bring you into my world, the world of a woman who notices things and cares about what she sees.

I have always loved animals. My parents instilled in me a love of nature from an early age. I can remember watching the building of a block of maisonettes, we were later to move into, from the flat we lived in. Building work had stopped on one section and someone had given my Dad a pair of binoculars so that we could use them to see the reason why. I could have been no more than two years old when, guided by my parents, I looked through the binoculars and saw a mother blackbird sitting on her nest. Over the following weeks we watched as the eggs hatched and she raised her chicks. I do not remember seeing them fledge but seeing that bird sitting on her nest is one of my earliest memories.

Animals have also been a part of my family. My mother told me stories of her own father, who sadly died before I was born. He was a London butcher, providing the local community with meat during the Second World War whilst breeding and raising rabbits at home. Mum regaled me with stories of a pen, in their back yard, filled with tiny bunnies. She described the different colours of the baby rabbits' fur, the names of those colours, the patterns they made when you blew on the fur and how the rabbits all had different characters. Through her eyes I could see them scampering around as she cleaned out their cages and fed and watered them. I envied her that experience although would have been appalled by what was most likely their fate; there was a war on after all.

My grandfather also bred and showed budgerigars. I still have a selection of the budgerigar shaped button-hole badges that he was awarded at various shows. I was fascinated by them, by the colours of the birds and by what they meant. There is a photo of my mother, aged about nine, standing proudly in front of one of the aviaries in their back yard. It was hardly a garden being part of a tenement block in south London in the 1920s.

Above: Mum in front of the aviary

Loving and caring about animals is in my genes. I grew up in South East London in the 1960s and 70s. My parents instilled in me a responsibility towards animals. If you bring an animal into your home, you have the responsibility to look after it properly; to care for it and treat it with respect. As a newlywed couple my parents had owned two Scottie dogs, a mother and daughter. My Mum never forgot what it was like to return from the vets carrying only the collar, having had to have one of them put to sleep. She had to make a repeat trip for the other dog several months later. The pain of their loss was so great that as children we were not allowed to own a much-wanted dog. It is only now, having cats of my own, that I truly understand the enormity of the loss she must have felt. For my parents, as it is for me, they were not 'just animals' but a huge part of the family.

However, growing up we were allowed to have a yellow budgie called Joey (weren't they all?) who lived, way above the ground, in a cage hanging on a stand. He was allowed out during cage cleaning time and would tweet excitedly as he flew around the living room landing in inaccessible places from where he could tease us come catching time. He would perch on my Mum's fingers when she fed him, and he happily spoke a few words too.

He once told my Nan to 'Sit down!' and she was so startled that she did just that.

I also had a beautiful goldfish called Winnie. She was orange with a white fan-like tail. Winnie inhabited a tank with Charlie, my brother's goldfish. We kept them for many years, exceeding the short life predicted by the pet shop owner who sold them to us, mostly due to my Dad's excellent care. I would watch him cleaning the tank as they swam about in a bowl on the kitchen draining board. Dad would ensure the clean water in the fish tank was the same temperature as the 'old' water in the bowl, before they were put back in the tank. We even took them on holiday with us. My Mum would sit in the passenger seat of my Dad's Anglia or Ford Escort, a large sweet jar clasped between her knees as the fish sloshed about inside. The lid of the jar had been punctured with a bradle to provide air holes for the journey. The fish tank would then sit on the kitchen counter in our 1960s rented self-catering bungalow for the duration of our stay. When the holiday company said, 'no pets' they clearly didn't mean goldfish.

Above: Nan, brother David, Marion, Dad, Uncle Jack and Aunt Alice with Susie the poodle.

Although we could not have a dog my Aunt Alice and Uncle Jack did have one, a black poodle called Susie. She was a delight. Whenever we went to stay with my Aunt and Uncle, Susie would rush out to greet us. It was advisable not to wear shorts for that first meeting but I was of an age when shorts were all you wore and the scratches on my legs were merely proof of her excitement at seeing me again. At night, as we settled down to sleep, she would tour the house, the sound of her claws clicking on the lino, as she went from room to room, nuzzling any outstretched hand, making sure everyone was safe before she settled down to sleep.

As I grew up I my love of animals continued. I watched every episode of Daktari, Tarzan with Ron Ely, Flipper and Forest Rangers. They may have been in black and white, but I saw the colours of the exotic animals in my mind. I wanted to see lions, elephants and giraffes in Kenya. I wanted to swim with a dolphin. I wanted to own a dolphin and I could not understand why my parents would not let me keep one in the bath. I promised to look after it and clean out the bath each week. It seemed so unreasonable of them to say no. I had to console myself with an inflatable yellow dolphin instead and together we had many adventures in holiday camp swimming pools, saving the world as my kicking feet propelled us frantically across the pool. My dolphin would give a squeak whenever I squeezed his left flipper. Happy days.

When I received the Lady Bird book of African Mammals as a present one Christmas, I devoured it. There was information on one page and beautiful illustrations of the animals on the other. I set about learning the names of all the animals, their habitats and feeding preferences. When we visited Windsor Safari Park, I was able to put my knowledge to good use, but they had something else I was so desperate to see, bottlenose dolphins and Ramu the killer whale. I remember peering through a glass viewing window and Ramu swam over to peer back. The huge black and white sea mammal made eye contact with me. It was life changing stuff. I knew I loved these animals. I knew they had to be a part of my life. I also knew that keeping such beautiful living things in cages or small tanks could not be right. I clearly remember the indoor aquarium at Brighton and the dolphin shows held there. When the dolphins would leap from the water, they almost touched the ceiling. Fortunately, today the very thought of dolphin shows causes an outcry. How anyone thought dolphins should be kept indoors is beyond me. At the time we knew no better; now we are well aware of the stress such environments cause and no cetacean should be kept in a tank.

I continued my love of nature and the natural world through my education. I studied Biology at University and received a First-Class Honours Degree from the University of London. I became a Science teacher and tried to instil a love the natural world into the minds of teenagers, harder with some than others. Not every child has parents willing to take them for trips into the countryside or walks through the park. I soon realised that a child's attitude to animals and care of the wider world were formed from their own experiences. My parents had taken us beyond our hometown. I was teaching children who had never seen a cow and so, on field trips, I tried, as my parents had, to pass on my enthusiasm and love for the world around me. We went pond dipping, took a trip in a boat to spot seals, scoured rock pools for crabs and shrimps and even rescued a sheep who had her head stuck in a fence.

My husband, Brian, was also an animal lover and it was this mutual appreciation of the natural world that brought us together. I promised myself that as soon as I could afford it, I would go on safari in Kenya. Ever since watching Daktari and Tarzan, which were ironically filmed in the USA, I had dreamed of going to Africa. For years I collected pages from holiday brochures, outlining particular tours and destinations, so I knew exactly where I wanted to go and what I wanted to see. I did not want to stay in fancy lodges and travel in a minibus. I wanted a land rover, camp chairs and a tent. Eventually I found the Dick Hedges Safari run through the tour company, Kuoni. I would be staying in a tent, travelling by land-cruiser and visiting the Masai Mara, Lake Nakuru and Samburu. Perfect. There was only one problem; it was not a trip I was confident enough to take alone and there was no one who could go with me. I mentioned this at work and Brian piped up, 'I'll go with you'. Apparently, he went home that evening and tried to figure out how on earth he would be able to afford it, but afford it we did.

In August the following year we flew to Kenya. A bumpy journey, on the worst unmade road I have ever travelled on, took us from Nairobi to the Masai Mara. Almost immediately we spotted zebra and hartebeest, but my eyes brimmed with tears when I first spotted elephants. I thought I would be overwhelmed by the millions of wildebeest, seeing a lion's kill, or hearing them roar but it was elephants, living free, that made me cry.

The safari was a dream-come-true. We were up before dawn each day with only enough time to grab a mug of tea before heading out in the vehicles. I was fascinated that in the middle of nowhere you would suddenly smell coffee, that sound travelled so far when unencumbered by buildings and that the amazing tan I thought I had was just a thick layer of dust. My tan washed down the sink when we stopped at Keekorok Lodge for refreshments. I do not think I have ever felt quite so much like a street urchin as I did watching the dust slide off my arms and swirl around the plug hole as American ladies, clad in designer safari suits, reapplied their make up over by the mirror.

Out on the plains all the animals from my Ladybird book of African Mammals were there to see and photograph, but it was the plants and invertebrates that made me realise I was a stranger in a strange land. I knew not to try and pet a lion but had no idea what that strange looking beetle was or whether it was safe to brush against a plant. I still had so much to learn.

Above: Marion and our Masai Mara tent

From the Masai Mara we travelled overland to Lake Nakuru and north to the arid lands of Samburu. I will never forget the sights, sounds and smells of that amazing country nor the wonderful people we met; people who walk for miles every day just to buy the essentials of life and who smile and wave at strangers. From Kenya we flew to the Seychelles where we saw green turtles swimming in the clear blue Indian Ocean, the black parrot perched high in a tree and fruit bats flying across a sky filled with so many stars it was positively Biblical. Sitting on the beach at sunset, as the ghost crabs scampered on the sand, with the palm trees silhouetted against the sky, it was perfection. However, it was not quite the paradise we expected. Signs in the hotel warned us not to touch the fire coral, and to beware the dart of a cowrie shell. Later, as I swam in the ocean, I was lashed by the tentacles of a jellyfish. For two inexperienced travellers it truly was the holiday and experience of a lifetime.

Above: Brian in the Seychelles

Our next adventure was closer to home. I wanted to see seals and the nearest ones to our home, were to be found lounging on the sandbanks of Blakeney Point in Norfolk. We set off in Brian's car, for the long journey north, on arrival we parked at the foot of a huge sand dune and approached the car park attendant for local advice. Did he know where we could see seals? He nodded and pointed out across the marshes. Was it far?

"Three an' half mile, seem more like ten," he informed us in his broad Norfolk accent.

He was not kidding. It was one of those trips you laugh about once it is over. At the time as we jumped ditches, clambered through mud and gorse, got covered in sticky who-knows-what and pulled our walking-boot clad feet out of some primordial ooze, it was not as much fun as we had envisaged. However, we did, eventually, reach the seals and seeing them lying serenely on the vast sandy beach was worth all the effort to get there. I am sure there was an easier way to reach them, and I am still not convinced the car park attendant did not laughingly send us on the 'tourist route' but that would not have given us so many stories to tell later or the experience that brought Brian and I closer together

Next on my 'to see' list was orca and once again, thanks to my years of research, I knew exactly where they would be, Vancouver Island. It was long before the internet, so we headed to our local branch of Thomas Cook the travel agent and through them I arranged a bespoke trip. First, we would travel to Tofino on the west coast of Vancouver Island to see grey whales. The beaches were idyllic, the sunsets a photographer's dream, and Clayquot Sound was stunning, but the grey whale was less than impressive. We only saw the dorsal fin of one as it rummaged around for food on the seabed before producing a blow that filled the air with the smell of cabbages. It was wonderful to have seen it but I have to admit the whale took second place to the bald eagles. The trees and sky were full of these magnificent birds. They were easy to see when perched in a tree as their white head stood out against the green foliage. I was mesmerised and they remain one of my favourites tying only with a gannet as far as sea birds go.

From Tofino we travelled across the island to Telegraph Cove on the east coast. We drove for hours from Campbell River seeing nothing but trees, the occasional logging truck and more trees.

'It's just trees,' Brian said. 'Two and a half hours of trees.'

He was right; all you could see were trees. So, I bought a book of trees but when you are driving, they are not so easy to identify.

Telegraph Cove was beautiful. It is a boardwalk community which over the years has seen huge development but our first visit, and there were many over the years, was before all of that. It was there, as we walked along the board walk that surrounds a small marina, that I saw my first hummingbird. My British brain kicked into action and I thought it was a huge dragonfly! I had no idea hummingbirds could live that far north. Since then, I have seen many different species of hummingbird and every time it is a thrill. Hummingbird wings beat on average 50 times per second. I wish we had them in the United Kingdom.

To see orca, we motored out into Johnstone Straight aboard the Lukwa, Stubbs Island's purpose-built whale watching boat. I was excited, my camera at the ready, we were finally going to see Ramu's relatives. The water was flat, calm and grey. A cold fog had descended. We pulled our jackets tighter and scanned what we could see of the horizon, which in truth was not much. Our chances of seeing anything, let alone a killer whale, looked bleak. However, the people of Stubbs Island knew their job. After an hour and a half, with the fog having lifted, they stopped the vessel. A hydrophone was lowered into the water 'just to see what might be around'. We heard the plop, plop, of the water and listened. Nothing. We scanned the flat water around us. Nothing....and then, suddenly, weee-earrrrr. It was an orca's call. They are here! I could have cried. Ok, I did cry. I stood on the deck of the Lukwa with a silly grin on my face and tears running down my cheeks. Suddenly a large black dorsal fin broke the surface of the water followed by a blow of expelled air, then another smaller more curved fin appeared beside the male. It was so wonderful. So very, bloody wonderful. To this day whenever I first see a whale (and I know orca are members of the dolphin family) I cry. I am just so thrilled so see them. They do not have to show themselves when we are around and the fact that they do I find a huge privilege. Just being in their presence brings me an enormous feeling of calm. It feels as if I am exactly where I am supposed to be.

Above: Orca in Johnstone Strait

Over the years Brian and I have seen many more orca from Telegraph Cove including A5 or Holly, the whale I have adopted from the Whale and Dolphin Conservation society for over 29 years. We have been whale watching in Quebec, where we saw beluga and fin whale, in Nova Scotia where we saw Atlantic grey whales and on the west coast of Scotland where harbour porpoises played about our boat. One day I would love to see a Blue Whale. I cannot explain it and only people who feel the same can understand but whales and dolphins have always been my thing.

It was through Brian that I met Sasha. I was badly scratched by a neighbour's dog as a child. It was not the dog's fault , he was untrained and, in his excitement, jumped up at me scratching my neck with his claws but he frightened me all the same. I had been wary of dogs, and getting close to animals, ever since. When we went to visit Brian's sister in Canada, his brother-in-law picked us up from the airport, and as we drove home, he mentioned that we had to collect Sasha on the way there. Sasha turned out to be a small, black Yorkie-poo (a Yorkshire terrier/poodle cross). He had just been neutered and we collected him from the vet. Sasha was placed on the seat beside me. I was not happy at having to share the confined space with an unfamiliar dog. I was nervous but Sasha was small and vulnerable; looked sorry for himself and a little confused. When he tilted his head and looked up at me, his small black eyes met mine and my heart melted. I reached out a hand, gave him a scritch behind the ear (in the manner of Charlie Brown and Snoopy's 'scritch, scritch, scritch') and fell in love.

Sasha was the most amazing dog I have ever known. Whenever we stayed with Brian's family, I would take Sasha for a walk. We would take the trail lined with trees and bushes, that ran along the creek behind the house and he would sniff the pee-mails left by other dogs as I chatted to him or stopped to photograph the flowers or the occasional banded snail. Our route might include the small bridge over the creek or around the local streets. One time, as we walked along the nature trail, his ears shot up and suddenly a deer sprang out of the undergrowth right in front of us. On another occasion Sasha began to growl and grew agitated. I held his lead tight as a coyote loped by.

Sasha restored my trust in animals. I learned how to safely pick him up, to let him sit on me and soon trusted him enough to let him lick my hand. When the temperature soared as it often did in Ontario in the Summer, I would share an ice lolly with him. A bite for me, a piece for him, a bite for me, a piece for him.

Above: Sasha

As the years went by and Sasha grew older, our trip around the trail took a little longer, but I would stop and let him rest, sitting on the kerb beside him as he got his breath back. And then Sasha lost his sight. It was heart-breaking to see him bumping into furniture on our next visit. He had lost his confidence and would not go for walks anymore. He was a shadow of his former self and I had to do something to help him. I knew that there were blind dogs living a full life. I had seen them on television programmes and knew they utilised their other senses more to compensate for the one they had lost and so, that summer, I took it upon myself to get Sasha out walking again.

The first day I slipped on his harness he was wary. At this point I should say that I never just 'slipped on' Sasha's harness. That thing was my nemesis. There seemed to be so many wrong ways you could put the darn thing on a dog. I don't know who invented it but, whoever they are, they have a warped sense of humour. Once harnessed up we headed to the front door. As expected, Sasha did not want to go out. I talked to him gently, reassuring him that all would be well and that we would take things at his pace. He was clearly nervous and on the first day we got only a few metres from the house before he sat down and refused to move another step. I picked him up and we returned home. We tried again the next day and got a little further. On the third day Brian walked in front of us. Sasha seemed happier to have another member of the pack walking ahead, leading the way and we got as far as the bridge that crossed the creek. Every day we made it a little further and by the end of our stay Sasha was walking his old familiar routes as if there was nothing wrong with him, even barking at a German Shepherd dog he could no longer see. Although he is no longer with us, I will love him forever. Sasha's photo is on the bookcase as I write. I am just thankful that I was not the one who had to return home with just the lead.

Brian and I continued to enjoy travelling and our holidays always involved some element of the natural world. We planned our own trips and if we were wildlife watching only used animal friendly companies.

Seeing nature in the wild may be a controversial issue to some. It involves carbon producing air travel, has the potential to disturb the very animals you have come to see but it can also help conserve them. If animals are shown to have a financial value for the local community, then the community has a vested interest in protecting them and ensuring their survival. Ecotourism brings in money for health care and education, and, having seen the animal they came for, tourists are more likely to support conservation projects. Done well, it has a benefit for all.

I would never knowingly do anything that would affect the animals I love to see. With Brian, I have watched black bears and grizzlies in the Canadian Rockies, seen hundreds of Puffins on the Farne Islands and marvelled at eagles flying in the Highlands of Scotland. I've seen glaciers, lakes, mountains, sunrises over Lake Louise, learned to paddle a Canadian canoe and watched otters scavenge on a Scottish shore. I cried again when I finally saw sea otters in Monterey, California. I love being on the ocean. I am happiest surrounded by unspoilt country or sitting on a beach listening to the waves lap the shore. To me the natural world is a constant marvel we are duty bound to protect and it is to the natural world I turn to again and again when I am at my lowest ebb. And it was animals that saved me when my days turned darkest.

The Rescued Cat Who Rescued Me

She strolled across the lawn without a hint of fear. Mum and I sat in our deck chairs, enjoying a cup of tea and the summer sun, when out of the bushes a small, extremely thin, tortoiseshell cat appeared.

"Hello," I said, and she took that as an invitation to approach. Mum and I exchanged a glance and an unspoken question passed between us. *Do you know who this is? No, never seen her before.*

The cat drew closer. "Mew," she said and curled up, in the shade, under my chair.

"Well, hello, Mew," I replied.

Mew made herself comfortable, her tail curling round to cover her paws and she rested her chin on the grass. Mum and I continued our conversation, neither of us moving too much in case we disturbed our visitor.

After a while I took a chance and got slowly to my feet. Mew stayed where she was until I returned a few moments later with a saucer piled high with tuna.

Mew was instantly on her paws and, when offered, gobbled up the fish like a...well, like a starving cat. It seemed she liked tuna.

As we worked in the garden the next day, Mew appeared once more. She settled herself down under a chair and accepted another saucer of tuna. Over the next few weeks Mew became a regular visitor and Mum's constant companion in the garden. She would sit next to Mum as she did the weeding or stretched herself out on a patch of grass to be warmed by the sun as Mum dead-headed the roses. When I arrived home from work Mew would be waiting, having used that sixth sense that animals have, to know exactly when it was time for my car to appear. Mew would sit on the pavement with her front paws placed neatly together and watch as I collected my bag from the car.

"Hello, Mew," I would say.

"Mew," she would reply.

The question had to be asked; should we officially adopt her and take her into our home? Mew was clearly a stray, taking food from a neighbour as well as the tuna we offered. It was a big commitment to own a cat, but we loved her enough to do that for her. We were off for a fortnight's holiday but would make the decision when we returned.

On our return we went out into the garden to tackle the weeds that had taken advantage of our absence and seemingly grown at twice their normal rate. The bushes rustled and Mew appeared. She dashed down the garden clearly excited to see us before slowing to a nonchalant stroll as if suddenly remembering she was a cat and not supposed to care. We were equally pleased to see her and fussed her as she rubbed up against our legs, but things had changed. Mew was wearing a collar.

In our absence Mew had sort comfort elsewhere and a neighbour had adopted her. We were pleased she had found a permanent home, somewhere safe to sleep at night but sad that it was not ours.

However, Mew still visited every day. She enjoyed chasing the string I trailed across the lawn, sat with Mum when she read the newspaper and enjoyed a good brushing so much that her back would arch and her claws extend in utter pleasure. She kept Mum company when I could not and for that I was incredibly grateful.

Above: The original Mew

And then her visits stopped.

No one waited on the pavement as I drove up.

No one bounded over the fence when we entered the garden.

We missed our friend and feared the worst.

We spoke to our neighbour. It turned out that Mew, although that was only our name for her, was not well. Our neighbour carried her out of the house so that we could see her. She was now a wizened version of our beloved friend. Age had caught up with her. I was pleased to see Mew, but her condition broke my heart. I gave her a scratch under the chin and her tired eyes met mine as I sent her a silent message of love.

A few days later she passed away. I shed more than a few tears that day. Mew had won a special place in my heart. She was never 'just a cat', she was a friend.

Life continued, as it must, until one day I heard a crash in the kitchen and rushed in to find my Mum lying on the floor. I knew immediately I saw Mum's face that she had had a stroke. My Dad had died from a stroke just five years before. From the moment I heard that crash my world crumbled and my life changed forever. Mum had cared for me and now it was my turn to care for her. I spent days sitting beside her bed watching her foot twitch as her brain tried to find a new way through the stroke-damaged nerves. My brother and I encouraged her to speak, to grip a soft ball with her hand and to regain all the stroke had taken away. Mum came home with a list of exercises to perform to improve her movement. I would often find her walking up and down the stairs because that was what the physiotherapist had instructed.

Over the next few years there were more hospital visits. Mum suffered several mini strokes which eventually led to her developing vascular dementia. Vascular dementia is not curable. It is caused by reduced blood flow to the brain affecting mental abilities, mood and balance. I sat beside my mother as doctors tested the short-term memory of a woman who had been an amazing organiser and solicitor's clerk. I listened as she could not recall 'ball, tree, shoe', which had been spoken only minutes ago and as she tried to remember what year it was. On several occasions I arrived home to find her on the floor. It is hard to describe the fear and sense of panic I felt finding the woman I loved more than anyone in the world, lying helpless in the bedroom or on the floor of the bathroom. Sometimes my partner Brian was there to help me pick Mum up, at other times I needed the help of paramedics. Our home was soon filled with adaptations to help Mum move about safely. There was a new handrail for the stairs, several in the bathroom, a zimmer frame and a button hung around her neck for Mum to press should she fall or need help.

As the vascular dementia progressed Mum lost more and more of her abilities and eventually, she needed carers to help with her basic needs. The frustration she must have felt, trapped inside a body that was slowly shutting down, is unimaginable. It was heart-breaking to watch a once vibrant, intelligent woman become smaller and less able, but no less loved. My own stress levels rose, exponentially as Mum woke throughout the night or fell with increasing frequency. I reduced my working week as a teacher but eventually gave up my job in main-stream education because, despite the suggestion of many of the senior staff, I had no intention of putting my Mum into a home. I cared for her as best I could because I loved her so much. The pain of watching someone you love fade is a pain beyond anything you can imagine.

In 2014 Mum passed away at home with my brother and I holding her hand.

My home was a hollow shell filled with only memories, handrails and other adaptations that were constant physical reminders of all Mum had suffered and of the woman who was no longer there.

In my grief I took to working in the garden. It was too soon to tackle all that needed to be done in the house. I could not face sorting through Mum's personal belongings. What right did I have to throw away things that had meant so much to her? It felt like an invasion of her privacy to look through the keepsakes of her life with my Dad before I was even born. I felt closer to Mum outside, pruning the roses she had planted, tending the plants she had grown from seeds or cuttings. I did not want to sit beside an empty chair, so I went out and started digging. I know now that bacteria in the soil help to raise our mood by triggering the release of serotonin and cytokines. Much research has been carried out into the value of gardening, and interaction with the soil, on our mental health. At the time I only knew that being in the fresh air helped and that being surrounded by nature has always made me feel happy. I relax with plants and animals around me. In my darkest times an image of waves lapping on a sandy beach comes to mind as if the sea is calling me to ease my worries. A beach is the place I find true solace. I know what helps me and I set to work in the garden, releasing some of my grief-fuelled anger and frustration as I plunged a fork into the ground and created a vegetable plot. I put up some bird boxes and an insect house. I painted the fence. I planted flowers. I breathed in the fresh air and little by little, I healed.

And then, not long after Mum had passed away a small tortoiseshell cat appeared, from the behind the bushes, in my garden. She wandered up to me without a hint of fear. I stopped what I was doing and crouched down.

"Hello," I said, keeping my voice as calm as I could.

She put her two front paws up on my knee. "Peru," she purred.

"Well hello, Peru," I replied. She looked so much like Mew it was uncanny. She appreciated a scratch under the chin and happily followed me around the garden supervising whatever I chose to do. "Are you hungry?" I asked when I deemed it was time for a cup of tea. She made a sound which I took to mean 'yes'. Disappearing into the house I returned with Mew's saucer, piled high with tuna. The tortoiseshell cat gobbled it up.

Above: Early photo of Mew 2

This new cat looked so much like Mew. It was not surprising that having only recently lost Mum, my mind would consider the possibility that somehow Mum had sent this cat to comfort me, or to let me know that she was keeping an eye on me. A lot of people find a robin turns up in their garden after a loved one passes away, clearly, I was getting a cat instead.

"Are you, Mew?" I asked, knowing full well that she could not be. "Did Mum send you?" Of course, the cat did not reply, there was a plate of tuna to consume and yet, crazy as it may sound, I felt as though Mum *had* sent her. I'm a trained scientist, a science teacher and I like evidence, although science cannot explain everything, but sitting in the garden looking down at this beautiful tortoiseshell cat I was willing to cast logic aside and go with what my heart needed; the strong belief that my Mum was still watching over me and this little creature was here to let me know that.

Weeks and months passed. Mew 2 as I had taken to calling her was a constant visitor to my garden although where she disappeared to at night I did not know. I fed her every day and when winter came, made a shelter out of a metal tub and lined it with a cushion and towels. I had never owned a cat so had no idea if this was adequate. Thinking back on it now, I am horrified to think of her out there in the cold and rain but at the time I was doing what I thought was best for her. I thought I was in no position to look after a cat and I assumed someone owned her. Today there are four purpose-built shelters in my garden for any stray cats that visit. If I had the time over again, Mew would have been in my house that first summer, but then what followed would never had occurred.

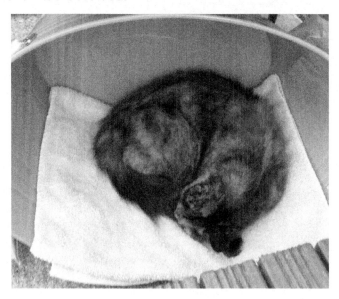

Above: Mew in the homemade shelter

The number two in Mew's name was soon forgotten and she became just Mew. Her coat grew thicker, and she made it through the toughest time of year. When spring and summer returned, she was always there when I appeared in the garden, always sitting nearby, watching me dig or plant or weed. Mew curled up in the flowerpots, chased invisible things through the vegetables and in keeping me company gave me someone else to care about, someone else at home to love.

Abovet: Mew wins me with a gaze.

One day Mew came and sat beside me on the garden bench and then without another thought climbed onto my lap, walked round in a circle, settled down with her head in my hand and fell asleep. Fortunately, because of all Sasha taught me, I was relaxed enough not to be startled, not to panic. To have an animal place themselves in your care at their most vulnerable moment, to place her head in my hand, was truly humbling and the bond between us was sealed.

Above: Mew sleeping on my lap in the garden

"Would you like to be my cat?" I asked as she lounged on my lap. I knew it was a big commitment; one I would not venture into lightly and just like with Mew the First, I was going on holiday soon. "When I come back, we can talk about you moving in, what do you say?" Mew shifted on my lap as if to say, okay.

When I returned from holiday, I was having the kitchen and bathroom renovated. Brick dust filled the air. Boxes were piled high in every room. Men with hammers and drills and big boots were stomping about. It was hardly the best conditions to welcome a cat into your home. Mew waited patiently in the garden and ran excitedly towards me when she saw I was home but once again things had changed.

This time there was no collar, but Mew was fatter. Her teats were pink and exposed.

"Are you pregnant?" I asked.

Above: A pregnant Mew

Mew looked up at me and our eyes met. As crazy as it sounds, I felt something pass between us. A woman-to-woman thing. She was not sure what was happening to her, but she was asking another woman for help. How could I refuse?

I still did not know if Mew belonged to anyone and had just been visiting all this time. Online advice suggested I attach a paper collar around her neck and write on it, asking the question, 'Does this cat have an owner?' Mew stood still as I attached the piece of paper around her neck and fastened it with some tape. She wandered off and I waited for a reply.

The next day when Mew appeared the collar was gone. Hmm. I fashioned another one and attached it. Off she wandered. Once more she returned without it. Had Mew's real owner removed it? Did they not want me to know that she was owned? Third time lucky? I made a new one, secured it around Mew's neck and watched as she strolled to the bottom of the garden and, with a few scratches of her paw, tore it off with a quick flick of a back paw. Well, that explained things. Mew looked at me as if to say, 'I want to stay here'.

There were no posters of missing cats in the area but there was one more thing I was willing to try. She might be microchipped. I would need a box to take her to the vet and they would also be able to confirm she was pregnant. I stood in the pet shop looking at the various sizes and styles of pet carriers. How big was it supposed to be for one cat? A friendly shop assistant suggested a cardboard carrier instead, the type they put a kitten or a rabbit in when you buy it and take it home. It was an excellent idea and much cheaper. So, armed with my cardboard carrier I returned home.

"I've bought this to take you to the vet," I explained to Mew as I did a bit of origami and turned the flat pack into a box shaped carrier. "We need to see if you have a microchip."

Mew looked up at me as she sat in the garden and then she grimaced.

"We have to find out once and for all if you belong to anyone," I informed her. "It'll be okay, honest."

She grimaced and yowled. Yes, it was definitely a yowl.

A pool of watery stuff appeared beneath her.

"Er, Mew are you...?"

She looked confused. Her breathing was rapid, and her eyes pleaded with me for help.

"Right," I said with more confidence than I felt. Remember, I had only ever owned a goldfish before, and Winnie never gave birth. Mum always looked after Joey the budgie and well...this was not something I had trained for. However, I sprang into action. A newly acquired black garden storage box was turned on its side and some towels laid across the bottom. The lid was propped alongside in a manner reminiscent of the old-style wooden pencil boxes, so that it could be slid open or closed. I turned to tell Mew what I had done but she already knew and walked inside. I sat outside with a pile of towels and a bucket of water; I have never had a child of my own, but I had watched births on TV, I was ready.

Fortunately, my help was not needed. Mew gave a few more yowls and then all was quiet. I waited until I could not wait any more, the silence was deafening.

"Can I see?" I asked as I gently tilted the box lid back. Mew looked up at me. Lying beside her on the now bloodstained towels were three damp kittens. Tiny tails stuck out the back of slick bundles of fur. Mew licked one of her babies. "Oh, Mew, they're beautiful."

But what was I going to do now?

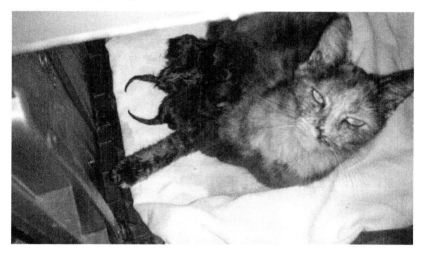

Above: Mew with the new-born kittens

My house was still a mess of brick dust, exposed floorboards and all-round chaos due to the renovation work. I had never looked after kittens. What was I supposed to do? I placed food outside the box and Mew would come out to eat it before being summoned back inside by the sound of mewing from one of her babies. She was an amazing mother keeping a constant eye on her tiny offspring, licking them clean and laying back as they suckled for milk. She instinctively knew what they needed.

Above: Mew with the kittens in the makeshift birthing den

In the few brief peeks I had taken of the kittens, I had identified them by their markings. One looked like a tiny tiger and was quickly and obviously named Tiger. Another had a stripe down the nose. So, for a time we had Stripy Nose and the third? The third I had only seen the bottom and tail of as this kitten had their head constantly buried into Mew in search of food. This kitten was growing the fastest too and so was eventually named Tubs.

Above: Mew's kittens

Above: Tiger

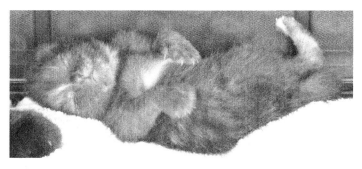

Above: Stripy Nose

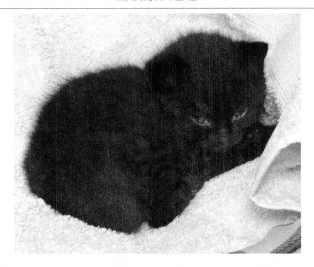

Above: Tubs

The question remained as to what I was going to do with them all. I had only just accustomed myself with taking Mew into my home, what was I going to do with three kittens? What did cats need? How much would they cost to keep? Would I have to change things in my home? Could I have keepsakes on shelves anymore? Would cats knock everything off and scratch all the furniture? What about my lovely new kitchen and bathroom? Were they doomed before I had even used them? If I was taking Mew and the kittens into my home, I was going to do things properly. I owed it to the cats to treat them right. I could not sleep, worrying about what to do. I wanted to keep them, but I did not know if I could; I did not know if I could cope with all the changes I would have to make.

One thing was certain, I was going to keep Mew but what did people do when their cats had kittens? From my newly gained knowledge, thanks to a lot of internet searching, it was clear that whatever happened mother and kittens were not going to be separated for some time yet. At some point Mew and the kittens would have to come inside the house. Where were they going to stay? Should I allow them full run of the house? If not, how do you contain a cat? I researched on the internet again and discovered a large pet play-pen that could be zipped up to contain Mew and all three kittens. I sent away for it and cleared a space in the front room in preparation.

What else would I need? A litter tray. How do you get a cat to use a littler tray? The kittens could be taught but would Mew use it? Did cat poo smell when it was in your home? When do kittens eat solid food? Would Mew teach them? Would I have to? The internet was a wealth of information and a confusion of advice.

And then it rained. Heavily. I placed a tarpaulin over the storage box Mew and the kittens were living in. It worked for a while but when I opened the box later, to check on Mew and her family, the towels were wet. Mew took charge of the situation and made a decision; she picked Tiger up in her mouth and carried him into my house.

"Mew, no!" I said. "You can't take him inside yet." I picked up Tiger, who was such a small bundle of tabby fur and returned him to the box where I had now laid a fresh, dry towel. Mew was having none of it. If I would not let her take Tiger indoors then she would take a different kitten. She picked up Stripy Nose, the tortoiseshell, and carried the kitten inside.

I sighed and recognised defeat. "Okay," I said. "But let me set the play pen up first."

Mew continued to carry the kittens into the house and found a suitable corner to keep them in as I busied myself preparing their new accommodation. When it was set up, with litter tray, cat bed and tiny scratching post, I moved them all in.

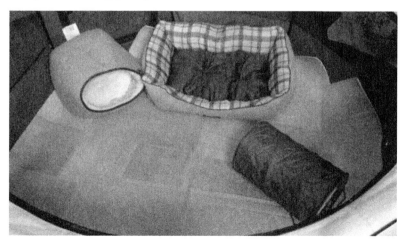

Above: The cat pen

Above: The kittens learn about litter

I now had four cats living in my home! What on earth was I thinking? I was thinking, I am in love and enjoying every minute of life with Mew and her kittens.

When the kittens' eyes finally opened, they were the most beautiful colour blue. They were the cutest kittens I had ever seen, they were the only new born kittens I had ever seen, and they were mine and Mew's. They toppled as they learned to walk. They practised pouncing and chasing. They began to show their personalities and their gender seemed obvious too. Tiger and Tubs were gorgeous boys and the third kitten with the stripy nose was a girl. I named her Jem after my Mum's initials, June Ethel May. Mew taught them to use the litter tray and would feed them regularly, their little noses pressing into her side to find the milk.

Above: Tubs

Above: Tiger

Above: Jem

I read everything I could on bringing up kittens. I had to socialise them, so they needed to be picked up and cuddled, which I was more than happy to do. Tiny paws walked all over me. It was heaven. I loved them all as if they were my own children. The strength of my feelings for them and how protective and maternal I felt towards Mew surprised me too. I have never been a baby person; never felt the desire to hold the baby a new mum shows you. 'Yes, very nice but wouldn't you prefer a puppy?' I had only ever imagined myself with a son aged seven, but they do not come that age and if you wanted one, with your genes in it, you had to grow your own. With Mew I found my maternal hormones on turbo. I had babies to protect.

Above: Mew and 5-week-old kittens sitting on me

And then I discovered I was allergic to flea bites. Mew presumably had them in her fur when she was pregnant, and they had come inside the house, hidden in her coat, and were now living in my home. Fleas! In my house! In the carpet. On the furniture. That thought alone was horrendous and had me itching, but when I discovered I had twelve highly itchy bites on my legs I needed help. The bites drove me mad and kept me awake at night. They became infected when I scratched them in my sleep. What was I to do? Would I be able to keep any of the cats? I was prescribed antihistamine tablets and lotions from the doctor. Colleagues thought I was mad to be keeping the cats when they were causing me so many problems, but it was not the cats' fault that I was allergic, and they were my responsibility now. You do not give animals away simply because they have become an inconvenience.

I took the cats to the vet. The kittens were an instant hit, and I felt a sense of pride that the little bundles of fur were mine and that I had helped to give them a safe start in the world. I had guessed correctly about their genders too. They were given a flea treatment that was safe for kittens and a nursing mother cat. It seems so many products out there cannot be given to a female cat if she is pregnant or feeding her young.

I bought flea traps with lights to attract the little devils and set them up in every room every night. I sprayed the carpets and furniture with flea killer I applied lotion and took antihistamines. The battle was on, but the cats were staying. I had invited Mew into my home. There was no way I was kicking her out now.

The next stepping-stone was to make sure the kittens switched from mother's milk to solid food. I sat holding pieces of food up to their tiny lips. Tiger did not want to know. Jem, being Dora the Explorer, ran off but Tubs...Tubs gobbled up the food first. He was living up to his name.

Then disaster struck. Tiger fell off the windowsill when exploring the room. He yelped and limped away into a corner. I watched him move. He was limping badly. What to do? If it was a child, you could ask them how bad it hurt and to tell you if the pain grew any worse, but you cannot do so with a cat. I searched for a vet. There was a local one open on a Sunday so into the carrier went Tiger and off we set in the car.

It was dark when I pulled into the forecourt of the veterinary practice. As I opened the car door to remove the cat carrier a cat strolled out of the vets and headed towards us.

"Hello," I said to the cat. "I've brought a kitten. He fell off the windowsill and has hurt his leg." The cat investigated the carrier, giving Tiger a look and a sniff, and then turned and headed towards the door. "I guess we should follow you," I said and picked up the carrier.

I followed the cat into the building where the receptionist explained that we had been greeted by Duncan, the veterinary cat. I suppose we had had the cat-scan already. Fortunately, Tiger was not badly hurt and only needed a painkiller and an anti-inflammatory. It was then I discovered how expensive an out-of-hours vet visit can be. We were definitely going to need some pet insurance. I know now that I could have waited until my own vet was open the following day, but I was like a new Mum and had so much to learn.

And then came the question I had dreaded; what was I going to do when the kittens grew up? I was keeping Mew, of that there was no doubt, but I had to be honest with myself, I could not keep four adult cats. Which kitten would I keep? I adored Tiger. He was a beautiful kitten and we bonded when he was injured. Everyone loved Tiger.

Above: Tiger in my lap

My brother had already expressed an interest in Tubs, so I had prepared myself for him to leave but what about Jem? Could I take a little girl away from her mother?

Above: Jem and Tubs

Above: Mew, safe at last

It was a heart-breaking choice to have to make. In an ideal world I would have kept them all, but I had neither the space nor the funds to do so. And then a lovely couple were found who would take two of the kittens. I made the hardest decision. Tubs and Tiger went together to a new home. Jem and Mew stayed with me. I could not take a little girl away from her mum. I was so thankful the brothers could stay together and there was another mother-daughter combination living in my house, it seemed appropriate.

Mew and Jem are now indoor cats because I found the flea bites made me quite ill at times. They sleep on my bed at night, greet me when I arrive home from work and Mew loves to cuddle on my lap. I would not be without them. I love them more than I could ever tell them, although I tell them every day. I am now a crazy cat lady through and through and proud of it. Some say I rescued Mew and her kittens, but in truth, she rescued me, and although I did not know it at the time, in the years, ahead I would need Mew's comfort even more.

Above: Jem and Mew

Before Lockdown

A Time of Crisis

Chirpy house sparrows flitted between the trees and the fat ball feeders, a herd of ramshorn snails chomped their way majestically, like a herd of wildebeest, across the algae on the bottom of the pond and three local cats snoozed in the sunshine. I knew what lived in my garden during the day but what went on at night? Did I have a hedgehog? I had not seen one for decades but, maybe there was one out there wandering about once darkness fell and I just had not seen it. I lived in hope.

Amusing myself on the internet I had seen lots of people on various Facebook groups, posting videos and pictures of animals captured on their trail cameras. Having come down in price they were no longer just the prerogative of a wildlife documentary maker, ordinary people could easily set them up and snoop on their garden visitors. I did a little more research, chose one I liked the look of and sent away for a camera. Once it arrived, I selected a suitable position in the garden, close to where debris from the bird feeders fell, put down some cat food and turned the camera on. For the first few days I had a lot of photographs of the local stray cats, Spot, the black and white one, Tux, the tuxedo cat and Hunter, the occasionally aggressive tabby. Then there were the pigeons both wood and feral, an opportunistic magpie and a couple of crows who I named Russell and Jo. A mouse appeared looking remarkably like the one in The Gruffalo but there were no hedgehogs. I continued to put down food and study the images captured on the camera over the following days.

And then there was a fox.

Or were there two foxes? It is difficult to tell foxes apart if all you see is a piece of their tail, the occasional foot, and parts of their faces. They would appear side on, stare at the camera and be gone in a flash as if they had no intention of helping me identify their gender or being able to tell them apart. I read that foxes like eggs, so I put one out for them. My camera, set on photo mode, took a photograph of the egg on the ground and then a photograph of the ground with no egg. Whoever had taken it was extremely fast and camera shy, it also highlighted the drawback of the time lag on the camera.

As the garden visitors became used to the weird contraption that flashed a red light at them in the dark, they relaxed and began to stay for longer around the food. From what I could see the foxes looked healthy with luxurious fur and characteristically bushy tails but, were they male or female? I still had no evidence to come to a conclusion. Clearly, I was going to have to devote more time to studying foxes. It would pass a quiet evening, a relaxing way to unwind at the end of the day teaching....

And then my partner, Brian was rushed to hospital.

One-minute life was normal and the next I was following a blue-light ambulance through the lanes of Kent, and then sitting in a hospital accident and emergency department stunned by the doctor's announcement that Brian had a large tumour growing inside him. He would need an immediate operation to remove it. Brian was rushed into surgery that night for a lifesaving operation. I stood in Accident and Emergency holding his folded clothes, with his shoes resting on top, and watched them wheel him away. I had no idea if I would see him alive again. Everything faded into insignificance at the same time as every detail of that casualty department was etched in my brain, the row of plastic chairs, the posters on the wall and the tea trolley, kindly provided for patients and their relatives. All that mattered was that Brian survived.

He had been taken earlier that day to hospital suffering from sepsis and, when the gravity of the situation became clear, was 'blue-lighted' by ambulance to another hospital for more specialist treatment. I followed on in my car and then, in the middle of the night found myself alone with no idea how to get home. I did not have sat-nav, the man I loved was on his way to surgery and I was in shock. I made my way through the automatic doors that led to the outside world and stopped in my tracks. What was I going to do? Where was this hospital and how was I going to get home? Words flashed through my mind. Large tumour. Emergency surgery. Large. Tumour. I leaned back against the wall, my knees folded, I lowered myself slowly down the wall and sobbed my heart out. A lady from reception spotted me in distress and asked what was wrong. I mumbled some sort of explanation; she sympathised with me and gave me directions to the dual carriageway. Having pulled myself together I headed to the car park, climbed into my car, placed Brian's belongings on the seat beside me and drove home.

The following day when I arrived at the hospital Brian was in intensive care. I was elated to find him awake but groggy. Maybe things were going to be all right after all. But my optimism was soon dashed as Brian's breathing rate increased and I recognised the grey pallor of his skin that signalled the return of sepsis. He needed to return to surgery...now! If he did not have the operation his chances of survival were 10%. If he did have the operation, they were also 10%. Once again, I watched as they wheeled Brian away and this time there was even less chance of them wheeling him back.

But the odds were in his favour and Brian was returned to intensive care. Every day as I drove the 40 minutes from home to the hospital, I knew there was a chance he would die that day. The doctors had told me that. I never knew what I would find as I walked the, soon familiar, route into the hospital, down the steps and along the corridor. I arrived each morning at the Intensive Care Unit with a lump in my chest. I rang the bell and waited to be admitted into a world of beeping machines and I looked towards his cubicle preparing myself to see an empty bed. Every day I put on a protective apron and gloves, sat at Brian's bedside from 10am until 8pm, watching the highly skilled nurses tweek the medication entering his body through numerous tubes and recording data on a giant chart. I held Brian's hand, I talked to him hoping that, although unconscious, he could hear me, I told him he would get better, and I encouraged him to fight. He was on a ventilator and receiving dialysis. The doctor told me Brian might die when they removed the ventilator. I prepared myself for that eventuality. He survived. They said he might die when they took him off dialysis. As I drove to the hospital on the day they were due to remove the tubes, I was mentally planning Brian's funeral and, when I arrived, they had already taken him off dialysis and Brian was still alive. I channelled the strength of my maternal grandmother and my mother; from the women in my life who had lost family members in the First World War and were bombed out of their homes in the Second World War. If they could face such things, then I would be strong too.

Minutes turned into hours, hours turned into days of waiting and hoping. One afternoon, having completed the crossword in the newspaper and read all about insignificant world events, I sat holding Brian's hand, looking at the cannula inserted into a blood vessel. I moved my gaze to the white bedsheets and blue NHS blanket and saw the outline of a nun in their folded shape. It was so clearly a nun. I am not one of those people prone to seeing Jesus in a tortilla or Bob Marley in the toast, but this was a nun. Or, more specifically, Saint Bernadette. I am not religious, although I try to live by Christian values, but will admit to praying to any deity that would listen when I knew what was happening to Brian. Call it emotional trauma or wishful thinking, but this was definitely the outline of Saint Bernadette. I Googled her and sure enough the shape in the bedsheet looked like the image of the Saint in her funeral glass case. I later discovered that Brian had her book in his house, and I downloaded a version to read as I sat by his bedside. It did provide comfort, believing, however hard it was to explain, that someone else was fighting in his corner, someone else with perhaps a greater influence on the great unknown, than I had. I promised Saint Bernadette I would visit Lourdes if she was able to help. I will honour that promise one day.

Every evening I would make the trek along the hospital corridor, up the stairs and out through reception to my car. One evening I found myself overwhelmed and sank into a chair in reception. As I sat crying in the deserted hospital a man on his way to deliver medicine to patients at home, came over and asked what was wrong. When I told him, he asked if I needed a hug. I shall be eternally grateful to the kindness of that stranger. It was exactly what I needed; human contact and understanding. How strange that in times of crisis we reach out to others, even people we do not know. I also chatted to a woman as we sat in the waiting area for relatives of patients in intensive care. There was a strange camaraderie between us, we knew what the other was going through, the anguish of waiting, hoping, not knowing. There was no one else to do that for me. I spoke to my brother daily on What's App but it was not the same as having a person beside you, someone to get you a cup of tea or take the next watch.

However, every night when I climbed into bed Mew would be there. She began to sleep on my chest, her chin resting on the hand I placed above the covers. She would bump my nose with hers, as she settled herself down, as if trying to reassure me, and she remained there as I cried myself to sleep. Her weight on my chest was a comfort. Her whiskers tickling my face a delight. Brian had often said about Mew, it was nice to have another heartbeat in the house. He was right. Knowing she was there, being able to rest a hand on her fur and listen to her gently purring gave me strength. Jem also began to join us and chose a place by my feet. Mew was still on the bed, snuggled in beside me, when I woke the next morning. This became our routine. Every night when I arrived home from the hospital, they would greet me, every night they slept with me, every night they were my greatest comfort. I believe animals are receptive to the way we feel and perhaps the mother in Mew knew I needed her help. It was as if I had helped her and now she was helping me. It would have been even harder to make it through those dark days without Mew and Jem. They are my family. My life.

Eventually Brian was well enough to leave intensive care and they transferred him to a ward. The care he received as he recovered was second to none and the nurses were wonderful but, he was a shadow of his former self. He had horrific bed sores that had to be treated, his muscles had withered so much he needed help moving in bed and to be able to stand. Brian needed to gain enough strength to walk again and had lost four stone in weight by the time he finally made it home.

There followed further trips to hospital for scans, tests and meetings with consultants. The cancer could not be removed. I still remember the looks we were given when Brian's cancer was pronounced incurable and we were told that his care would be palliative. It was as if they were calling out 'Dead man walking!'. I hated it and hope that Brian did not see the pity in their eyes. I wanted to yell out 'He's still alive! There is hope! Give us hope!' I knew new drugs were continually being found or created. Others would have completed their clinical trials and await the legislation needed for them to be prescribed to patients. It was a matter of staying alive long enough for a treatment to be found that would prolong Brian's life. So please don't look at us as if there is no hope. It was hope that was keeping us going. We knew our time together was going to be shorter than we hoped but I do not give up, ever. Chemotherapy began and despite all our fears and all you see on television, the nurses were amazing, and he had few side effects. The hospital oncology unit became a familiar place to be. I bought us a hot chocolate from the café as we sat waiting for Brian's name to be called. Every chemotherapy session started with a jolly smile from the nurses, a check of his blood pressure and a joke or two. I sat beside him as the medication ran into his blood through a port surgically implanted beneath the skin of his chest. We had a new routine and we were making the best of it, staying positive. There was always the chance that a new drug would be discovered and licenced before they ran out of treatments they could use. For a while we had hope. We ventured out to create a new normal and Brian enjoyed having fish and chips at a local restaurant after a hospital visit, but everything revolved around the cancer treatment.

Then Brian developed sepsis again. He was taken back into hospital, treated with antibiotics and, when deemed well enough, sent home. The chemotherapy had to stop until he was strong enough to face it again. Sadly, sepsis was something he could not shake. It returned again and again, and he grew weaker after each bout. Every time he was confined to bed Mew would sit with him, laying alongside his leg as if she knew he needed her. One time when he was in hospital, he even dreamed she was there, lying on the bed beside him. He said that was comforting.

After 28 years together Brian and I were finally going to get married. We had always had our own houses and not lived together, as we had both cared for our parents, but it probably explained the longevity of our relationship. However, we both knew, although we never actually said it, that our time together was growing shorter. We wanted our love to be acknowledged officially. I wanted to be his wife, a role I had been filling unofficially for many years, and not 'just his girlfriend'. Brian wanted that too. "Come on, let's do this properly," he said, one day in August 2019, as he got down on one knee to propose to me. Of course, I said "Yes". Ed Sheeran's song 'Thinking Out Loud' was playing on the radio as I helped Brian back to his feet and I burst into tears as we hugged. We were sealing our love in law but we both knew why we were doing this. Brian was going to die. Brian wanted to know I would be taken care of, and I wanted to keep him a part of me forever.

I arranged everything for the wedding as I sat beside Brian's hospital bed during another admission for sepsis. As he lay there looking tired and grey I bought my dress and shoes from Amazon; if the dress was white and the shoes fit, I was happy. I booked the registry office which was next door to the hospital. There would be only four people in attendance. I ordered flowers for buttonholes and a bouquet for me in between trips to the supermarket for food and arranging lasting power of attorney. When the day of our wedding came, Brian was extremely tired, and I was not sure if he would be strong enough to go through with the ceremony. However, when he saw me in my dress his eyes welled with tears and he told me 'You look beautiful'. Then my eyes filled with tears too. What a pair we were.

I used Jem's old collar wrapped around the bouquet as my 'something borrowed and something blue', the taxi arrived, and we were off. We all sat down throughout the ceremony as Brian was too tired to stand and I had to help him put the ring on my finger; it was one he had had specially made for me on the Isle of Skye many years ago. I had worn it ever since on the third finger of my left hand and had had it adjusted so that he could slip it over my, now arthritic, finger. With my brother, David and my Mum's carer, Elsa as witnesses we were wed. We got the taxi home and Brian was so tired he went straight to bed to recover. I sat downstairs with my brother and Elsa drinking a cup of tea.

In the following days Brian grew weaker. He could hardly leave his bed and was in constant pain. After a day like something from a nightmare, he was taken into hospital suffering from sepsis once more and the doctor in accident and emergency told me "He could die tonight." His blood pressure was so low they had to cover him with a special inflated blanket to keep him warm. I sat alone once more, trying to process the finality of those words, realising that we had come to the moment I had been fighting so hard, for so long, to prevent. Brian told me "I'm not going anywhere" and "I adore you, Marion." I loved him so very much. He did not die that night, he died three days later. We had been husband and wife for just 55 days.

Loss knocks you sideways. That is an understatement. My whole world, my whole life, changed in that moment. The nurses at the hospital were extremely kind. One had telephoned the morning they knew he was going so that I could be there. I sat with Brian for almost three hours after he passed. I held his hand as it grew cold. Friends, who I had to force myself to reach out to, scooped me up. So many things that mattered before became insignificant. I struggled to face a life without the man who had been my greatest companion for almost three decades. I did not just lose my husband. I lost my best friend, the person I planned and spent holidays with, the one who gave me his opinion on paint colours for the walls, who spent Saturday nights with me, watched TV with me, was my Valentine, lit the candles on my birthday cake and phoned me every day to chat about our day. Now the phone did not ring at that same time every evening. There was no message welcoming me home. Everything. Every single thing in my life either ended or changed the moment Brian died and the person I turned to for comfort was the one I had lost. Grief opens a huge hole inside you, and I could physically feel the hollowness within me. Now there was no one to do the everyday things with. I was suddenly alone. As I grieved for Brian, I realised that selfishly I was also grieving for the life I had lost and the places I would never travel to again and the things I would never do again because they were things, I did with him. Nothing would ever be the same.

There is a busyness when someone dies that gives you something to focus on in those first few days. I had Brian's funeral to arrange, his house to deal with, his possessions to sort through and I would do it alone. I registered his death with the same registrar who had married us. I bought a coffin, I booked funeral flowers from the same florist who had made my wedding bouquet and I ordered a black version of my wedding dress and shoes. On the day of the funeral my brother David was amazing, taking charge of the things I had not thought of such as having enough seats for everyone who came back to the house and making sure the front door was locked. The funeral directors were lovely, and I was praised by a friend for having the strength to give the eulogy; it had never occurred to me not to speak about Brian. He was my husband, and I would have done anything for him.

After the funeral I had to decide what my new life would be like, what I wanted to do with the time I had left. Losing a loved one makes you acutely aware of your own mortality and it scared me. I was terrified of losing my brother and Mew and Jem. I was terrified of growing old and having no one to look after me the way I had looked after Brian. I was grieving and I was terrified.

My life was not the only thing unravelling at that time. Across the world another event was about to affect us all. In December 2019, Covid-19, a new corona virus originated in a food market in Wuhan, China. The market sold live animals and in other parts of the world we scorned them for such practices. We stood on our moral high ground and said it was inhumane, unethical, and therefore not surprising that someone had caught a virus. It was zoonotic, said to have crossed the species barrier and had apparently transferred from an infected bat, either to an animal sold in the market or, and there was more speculation about this, maybe the bat itself had been consumed. Who knew what the truth was? And then there were also rumours that the virus was man made. Something new and unspeakable manufactured in the laboratories of the Wuhan Institute of Virology. It was known to be studying the effects of coronaviruses. Some nodded, knowingly, that it had probably 'escaped' but whatever the truth, China was too far away to make this a problem for us in the west. Oblivious of what was to come we continued to plan for Christmas and our New Year celebrations.

My brother came to stay with me for Christmas but in truth it felt like any other day. Christmas lost its sparkle for me the day my Mum died. I still like the lights, the carols, and the bustle in the shops but the spirit of Christmas and the excitement are gone. I loved buying presents for my parents and watching the look on their faces as they opened them. My brother and I do our best to make the day special for each other but that childhood magic of Christmas with our parents has gone. Losing Brian made it even harder to bear.

January 2020

The Fox year- January

In January, for foxes, there are fights for territories and food. The resident dog fox and his vixen defend their territory. Calls can be heard as they establish the right to the gardens, fields, or woodlands that they call home. Foxes mark their territories too, leaving faeces or urinating to announce their presence.

January is also the peak of the mating season. A female fox is in oestrous for around three weeks but is only receptive to the male for between one and six days. The dog fox stays close to the vixen to ensure that it is he and not a rival who mates with the female and passes on his genes to the next generation. Gestation is between 49 and 58 days.

Snowdrops poked their heads above the frosty soil, to herald the arrival of a new decade. For my Dad's funeral we placed three flowers, picked from our garden, into the wreath on top of his coffin, so the time of their flowering is an indicator, to me at least, of how different one year is from another. Do they arrive earlier than that day at the end of January or after it? Their return reminds me of my father whilst bringing joy that warmer, brighter days are ahead.

As we welcomed the new year, Wuhan, China, a city of 11 million people, was placed into lockdown. No one was allowed out. People were confined to their homes. The shelves of food shops were empty. A BBC news reporter was seen in a respirator mask, reporting from deserted streets. Anyone on the streets was challenged by the authorities, anyone suspected of having the virus was taken away. What on Earth was happening? You would never see such a thing happen here...or would you?

The virus was spreading. It was no longer just in Wuhan but moving across China. How was it transmitted? Was it airborne? There were so many people suffering that the Chinese were building a new hospital and planned to open it in record time. If the virus had already left Wuhan, then what was to stop it being carried by someone on a flight originating from the city? Authorities at Heathrow airport in the United Kingdom began screening all travellers arriving from Wuhan. In Wuhan itself, schools were closed, and factories shut. That would never happen here, you could not close the schools and stop people working. Then two cases of COVID-19 were recorded in the United Kingdom. Other countries began to report cases, but these were probably people who had travelled from China, nothing to worry about, it was never going to spread to the general population.

It would all blow over.

But it did not.

It reached Europe. Italy soon had so many cases that its hospitals were struggling to cope. Doctors and nurses were shown working frantically to save people, intensive care wards were overwhelmed, bodies were piling up, it was getting out of control and then Spain found itself in a similar position. These were countries in Europe. Countries like ours.

February 2020

The Fox year- February

Although most of last year's youngsters will have dispersed some females stay and become family helpers. In this way they improve the chance that the genes they share with the mother and her offspring are passed on to the next generation. The helper gains shelter and shared food. In return the vixen gains a babysitter as well as another pair of eyes, alert to danger.

The vixen starts to prepare her den underground, possibly in a disused rabbit warren or abandoned badger sett, although in urban areas it is more likely to be under your garden shed. Then she settles down to await the birth of her cubs.

In February 2020, the UK Health Secretary introduced new powers to quarantine people. Quarantine? In the United Kingdom? Surely this was just for people coming into the country from overseas.

I was not concerned about the new virus. SARS had been a threat before but apart from having my temperature taken at Vancouver airport before boarding a flight, it had never affected me. I had more important things on my mind. I was surrounded by memories of Brian and our life together. Everywhere I looked there was something, a photograph, a memento or a mug to remind me of all that I had lost. I sought solace in the garden as out there I was not surrounded by the boxes of Brian's possessions I needed to sort through or the paperwork that needed my attention. I had made far too many phone calls informing someone that he had died. I was overwhelmed.

The garden was a place of mental safety; out there I could breathe. Leaves rustled, birds twittered, and flower buds formed.

I had seen foxes once more on the night camera, one even appeared to be giving me a grin, and I was keen to identify them if I could. It gave me something nice to focus on. A pleasant diversion from the endless heartache. Some days there was a definite feel of Spring in the air. The sun shone brightly and my mood was on the rise. On other days I pulled back the curtains to see the sky was grey and the fountain-bird bath covered in a layer of ice. I pulled on my flowery wellies and was soon outside bashing away at the ice with a rock, like some neanderthal cave woman. There are environmentally safe chemicals you can add to the water to stop it freezing and I have some, but I only ever remember that when I find the water frozen. I really should pay closer attention to the weather forecast.

Above: A grinning fox on the night camera

On Brian's birthday, a fox appeared in the garden, came close to the house and looked in the window. It had a scar on its temple just below its left ear, and I remembered that I had seen a fox with such a wound in the garden a few days before. It also had a bleeding wound on its lower jaw. This was clearly the same fox. It was unusual for a fox to be around during the daytime. We made eye contact through the window, and I said 'Hello'. The fox seemed interested enough to stay and look around.

I do not know what you feel about animals appearing after loved ones die. Robins are often associated with departed grandparents, when all they are really doing is looking for a mealworm. For a while butterflies took on a significance for me after I saw one in the garden not long after my Mum passed away. I still see Mew as a sign from Mum. I felt she had a hand in sending her to me. As a scientist I know it is just our way of comforting ourselves. As a grieving daughter I would like to think that Mum sent Mew to me because the original Mew had meant so much to us both and it was her way of sending someone to look after me and someone for me to love.

Brian and I rarely talked about 'after', such was my desire to keep him positive. I suppose we should have discussed it more, but it was not something he ever showed a desire to do and with everything he had to face I had no intention of pressuring him to do so. However, I told him that when he was no longer here, should he be able to send me a sign, he had to make it obvious. "I want to know it is from you," I said. At the time I did not remember that we both had an ornament of a fox cub in our gardens or that he had two statues of St. Francis of Assis. One statue was in his garden and the other beside the large open Bible he kept in his office. The very Bible I had hypocritically prayed at throughout his treatment. St. Francis is the patron saint of animals! And I did not think about it being his birthday when the fox appeared at the window but now, having built a relationship with Vix, I returned to the old photographs of her and noted the date of that first eye contact. I can hear Brian mumbling "When I send her a sign, she doesn't recognise it!" Whatever you think, I comfort myself believing Brian had a hand in Vix turning up that day.

Above: The fox with the scar appears at the window on Brian's birthday

Having seen the healing wound on the side of the fox's head I was now able to identify it on the night camera. It was clear I had at least two different foxes visiting my garden after dark, one with and one without the scar, as well as the various stray cats, two mice, that lived in a wood pile, and a rat. There was still no sign of a hedgehog. The camera was focussed on the area below the bird feeders, and this was clearly a well-used stopping point on the nightly rounds of many animals. Knowing I had foxes, I put out some cat food to see if they would eat that. They did. I bought some dog treats and left those out. Some were taken, some were left. So much for them being 'irresistible'.

Then the fox with the scar returned to the garden during the day. It looked larger, fatter than before. Or was it just fluffier? I knew little about fox biology at the time and had never really studied the ones I saw, just marvelled at how lucky I was to see them in my garden at all. I had heard mating calls at some point during the winter and there would be the occasional barks at night and squabbles between foxes but that was the extent of my knowledge. There had been foxes in my garden before. One year a mother brought her five cubs to visit. They spent an hour chasing each other, leaping in and out of the bushes and playing excitedly on the lawn. When she had had enough of them jumping on her and biting her tail, the vixen leapt over the fence and sat down for a rest on the grass in my neighbour's garden as the cubs tried to find a way to get to her.

On another occasion a young fox arrived with a battered football. I watched fascinated as the fox tossed the ball up into the air and chased it around the garden. It grasped the ball between its teeth and shook it roughly, as if it were its prey, before biting into it and releasing a cloud of fluffy kapok. I had no idea how much kapok was stuffed into a football but before long white pieces were covering the garden like artificial snow. It took me ages to clear it all up but the joy I saw on that young fox's face made the effort worth it.

Above: The fox with the scar looking fatter

On the penultimate day of February 2020, I went to Kew Gardens to see the Orchid display. It was the first trip I had taken alone since Brian died. It felt strange to be visiting somewhere on my own and to not be able to tell him about my trip or share the experience with him but, it was something I knew I had to get used to. This was my life now. I could not sit at home and do nothing. I needed to learn to venture out and have new experiences even if it meant experiences I may not always be able to share with someone. The orchids and the displays created by the gardeners at Kew were amazing, and I enjoyed photographing the gloriously coloured flowers. I had a wander around the gift shop, as I always do, before I left. I have a feeling my autobiography will be titled "Exit via the gift shop" or maybe that should be my epitaph. For some reason whilst there I was drawn to a small cuddly fox sitting on a self. I did not need it as I have more than enough cuddly toys, but it gave me comfort as I picked it up and held it. Maybe it was because I was on my own and needed some comfort, whatever the reason I bought the fox. Why a fox? Coincidence? Probably.

Above: Cuddly fox from Kew Gardens.

March 2020

The Fox year- March

March is the time of the year that most fox cubs are born. The average litter size is 5 cubs, and they are born blind, deaf and covered in a grey woolly fur. The cubs weigh around 100g, about the same as two chicken eggs. The vixen stays with the cubs for the first few days as they are unable to control their own body temperature. As she snuggles close to her young it falls to the dog fox to provide her with food.

Narcissi, tete-a-tetes or tiny daffodils, began to spring forth from the warming soil. Whatever you choose to call them, their spring green leaves and cheerful yellow flowers, reminiscent of Welsh bonnets, always bring a smile. Spring is here they seem to shout from beneath the apple tree, on roadside verges and in gardens throughout the land. The hyacinths follow, filling the air with a delicious, distinctive fragrance. The crocuses dot the garden in places I cannot remember planting them. The yellow ones seem destined to be eaten by the birds. And finally, the forsythia bursts into bloom, a starburst of yellow flowers appearing on bare branches. Bees began to buzz about as food is available once more. Spring green and yellow are the colours of new life, the rebirth of nature and a reminder that whatever happens in the world, life continues.

High up on the branches of the magnolia tree, tiny furry buds cracked open revealing waxy pink petals and the cup shaped flowers burst into view. Ring-necked parrakeets had eaten some but soon the tree produced a magnificent display of oriental beauty.

I have always been fascinated how flowers form. If you asked me to make a flower, I would cut petal shapes from pieces of paper and fold them together into a bud. Plants start from the inside out. A single cell divides by mitosis to form two, four, eight cells and so on until the cells begin to differentiate into the different parts of the flower. Some become petals, others develop into stamens and the carpel. Pollen and the ovule develop by a different form of cell division, meiosis, halving the number of chromosomes as they make the plants' sex cells. All of this takes place inside a tiny bud. Natural 'technology' surpasses anything we can produce synthetically. I remain awestruck every time I look closely at a flower and my garden was beginning to bloom with them.

As I sat in the sun the warmth on my skin was an added bonus. Oh, to feel the warmth again after the long cold days of winter. The Sun's rays gave a promise of heady summer days to come. There is that one moment in Spring when the light and temperature are just right, and I suddenly get a feeling that it is no longer winter; this is it; it really is Spring, and we are heading towards more hours of sunlight and warmer days. It gives my soul a boost. When the Sun moved lower in the sky the garden was filled with a golden light. Nature's beauty in a halo of gold.

The next time I saw the scarred fox it looked considerably scruffier as it climbed onto my small shed/storage box (from now on to be called the shedlette) and surveyed the garden. I watched through the French windows as it sniffed the air and had a good look around; eyes ever alert for signs of danger although I was not sure what counted as danger for a fox at that time and there certainly was not anything to worry about in my garden.

I caught glimpses of the fox, over the next couple of weeks; at one point eating the left-over cat food I put out for the strays and on another occasion drinking from my pond. I still did not know if the fox was male or female although there did not seem to be any obvious male parts below the tail. In truth I had not been looking that closely, I just enjoyed seeing it in my garden.

Above: The fox with the scar drinking from the pond.

I put out more dog biscuits and the fox either ate them or took them away. I assumed it was going to cache the food. If they have more food than they need, foxes will find somewhere to store the extra, which seemed like a sensible thing to do. It is the reason dogs bury bones in the garden, an innate need to save food in times of abundance, for when it becomes scarce. I started finding the fat balls, that fell out of the feeders, buried in my flowerpots or in the vegetable plot. Caching food is one of the reasons foxes get such a murderous reputation. Why do they kill all the chickens in a hen house and then not eat them? Do they enjoy killing things? The answer is no. They do so because instinct tells them to prepare for leaner times. They have no way of knowing if there will be more food in the same spot tomorrow, so they take what they can now and cache what they cannot eat. A fox, finding itself in a chicken coop is like a chocoholic at the Cadbury's factory. It might not be able to eat it all, but it is going to stuff its pockets full for later.

Above: The fox with the scar during a daytime visit.

Whilst I concentrated on the fox in my garden, the BBC news reported that the threat of COVID-19 was increasing. It was recommended by the UK government that the over 70s and those with underlying health conditions consider self-isolating. What did that mean? It meant staying home, avoiding contact with other people and only going out when necessary to buy essential items like food and toiletries. For some it meant not going out at all and arranging to have food delivered to their door. Was it really that serious? Other countries were failing to contain the virus. Hospitals were inundated with extremely sick people. Intensive care units were full. The main symptoms we were told to look out for were a high temperature, a new, continuous cough and a loss or change to our sense of smell or taste. People were panic buying toilet rolls under the misguided belief that we were going to run out. Apparently, the rumours began because the toilet rolls in Australia were imported from China whose borders were now closed. The toilet rolls in the United Kingdom were not going to be affected but that did not stop consumers emptying the shelves in supermarkets. Stores found themselves having to limit the number of rolls each customer could buy. The same applied to hand sanitizer which we were all being encouraged to use regularly. Hand washing became a national obsession. The sound of people singing 'Happy Birthday to You' could be heard in bathrooms across the land because it took 20 seconds to sing it as you washed your hands for the recommend time.

On 16th March 2020 the British Prime Minister, Boris Johnson advised the public against non-essential travel. Things were becoming serious. People suffering from the virus often had extreme difficulty breathing and it was feared we would not have enough intensive care beds for patients requiring ventilators. We did not have enough ventilators either. PPE, personal protective clothing, had become part of our vocabulary along with, pandemic, social distancing and self-isolating. We started to end conversations to friends and loved ones with 'stay safe'. Science fiction had suddenly become a reality. Rumours began to spread that there would be a national lockdown. Just like they had done in China, we would all be confined to our homes. Surely that would not happen in the United Kingdom, not in the twenty-first century.

At work we began to prepare for self-isolating. The staff downloaded Skype and Zoom to their computers, laptops and tablets. We contacted the parents of the children we taught to explain the plans we were making should lockdown be imposed and how we would continue to teach from home. Would they still want tuition via the internet? Would we be able to provide it? Did they have a device we could contact them on? Some families had nothing more than one smart phone for the entire family to use. For vulnerable students and those with special educational needs there were also safeguarding issues to be considered. Some children would still be allowed to go to school whilst the majority stayed home. It was all hands to the proverbial pump as we prepared for what might come: teaching and caring for our students in a different way and from a distance.

My scarred fox continued to visit. I knew a fox appearing in the day was not normal, at least not on a regular basis and every time it visited it appeared to be extremely hungry, eating everything that was available. Every morning I put out food my cats had not eaten the night before and topped it up with a little extra. Any stray that was passing was welcome to eat it. Now that I knew I had a hungry fox also visiting, I added dog food to my weekly shopping list and bought a few tins on my next trip to the supermarket. I emptied a tin under the bird feeders and watched to see what would happen. When the fox with the scar appeared, it ate it all. I enjoyed seeing the fox and it felt good to ensure it had a good meal. It was rewarding to be able to help.

Above: The fox with the scar eats up the dog food.

On 23rd March 2020, Boris Johnson, ordered a nationwide lockdown. It was really happening. The entire population of the United Kingdom was told to stay home and only go out for essential groceries or to take no more than an hour's exercise a day. It was surreal and yet it was our new reality. There were fears as to how we would cope. What about people living alone? What about the elderly? How would vulnerable people get food? What about people's jobs? Would they be paid? Would they still have to pay the mortgage even though they were not able to work? There were so many unanswered questions to an unprecedented event and people were frightened too. A sense of foreboding filled the land and we waited to learn how the British Government would help us survive as we complied with the rules.

I had just begun to make a new social life for myself since Brian's death. I was forcing myself to say 'yes' to invitations to go to the theatre or for a walk in the woods. I was writing down events in the calendar for later that year. Now I had to stay home again. I had to cross out dates in the diary. I was on my own again, isolated once more. Locked down at home.

Lockdown Begins

The Self Isolating Bird Club

Self-isolation and social distancing were suddenly common vocabulary. Millions of people found themselves working from home, whilst sitting in their pyjamas or tracksuit bottoms. For many that meant learning how to contact others via Skype or Zoom, which often involved a lot of shouting at the screen, waving to colleagues, telling people to 'press unmute' or 'I can hear you, but I can't see you'. Work colleagues gathered on Zoom conference calls like the beginning credits of the Brady Bunch or The Muppets, but you had to be of a certain age to appreciate that reference. We were suddenly seeing into the homes of television presenters, government ministers and our work colleagues. Instead of listening to what they were saying we were eyeing up their bookcases, wondering if they had really read that large volume by Tolstoy and critiquing their home décor. We began looking behind us to evaluate our own background to determine if it was up to scratch. Books were repositioned on shelves to make us appear more well-read than we really were, new paintings were bought and hung and that vase, given to us by Aunt Mabel, was replaced with a potted plant. And then there were the children. Working from home for many also meant being surrounded by toddlers and there were several amusing incidents where a man in a suit was interrupted by a small child wanting Daddy's attention.

Stay home, protect the NHS, save lives, became the mantra. We were doing this for the common good. It was a nationwide act of altruism. We did not want the National Health Service to be overwhelmed by the number of people suffering from the virus. The most severely affected would need to be on a ventilator in intensive care. People were going to die. It was predicted that the number of deaths from the coronavirus could rise to 250,000 but it would be considered a success if we could keep it to 20,000 deaths. They were frightening numbers. Plans were afoot to turn the Excel Centre, in London, into a Nightingale Hospital capable of housing hundreds of patients on ventilators. Doctors and nurses were already exhausted and having to wear PPE all day made their job even harder. People could also be asymptomatic, have the virus and not know it. We did not know who had it or who might be unaware that they were passing it on. There was no test for it. No vaccine and no cure.

People were encouraged not to sit and worry but to use their newfound time at home to learn a language or to play a musical instrument. Some took up needle-felting or knitting, others chose yoga or worked out with television presenters. Those long-awaited DIY projects could not be done because shops were closed and unless that paint sitting in a tin under the stairs was still viable, painting the ceiling would have to wait. This was finally the chance we had always longed for to clear out the spare room, read that book, or declutter the garage.

Many, like myself sought comfort in their gardens. It was a time to appreciate the natural world on your doorstep. Chris Packham, the naturalist, and television presenter had started The Self Isolating Bird Club page on Facebook as a way for fellow nature lovers to connect during lockdown. There were lots of like-minded animal lovers there, not just bird watchers. I joined and posted a few of the photos I had taken of birds in my garden. They could not compete with the amazing images of swooping barn owls and red kites but that was not the point. It was about belonging and sharing your love of nature, not competing for the best photograph. If we were going to be on our own why not link up with others who shared our love of the natural world?

With millions of people isolated at home for possibly twelve weeks or more there was a justifiable fear that mental health issues would rise too. Being out in nature was known to benefit our mental health, so time in the garden would be good for us all. A connection with nature became vital to so many.

I was now calling the fox with the scar, Vix, because it was clear, from a closer look, that she was a vixen. She appeared regularly over the next few days, sniffing out tasty morsels, sometimes burying a fat ball in the flowerbeds and I made sure there was always some food out for her. She was such a beautiful creature.

Now that I was working from home and teaching by Skype, I could keep an eye on the garden to see when she appeared.

Above: Vix feeding in the garden.

When I spotted Vix on the night camera, she had a surprise in store for me. On her underside there were prominent nipples. Vix was lactating. She had not been fat or fluffy, she had been pregnant and was now a nursing vixen. That explained her constant hunger but where was her den and how many cubs did she have? I had no idea. When she disappeared over the garden fence her life beyond it was a mystery.

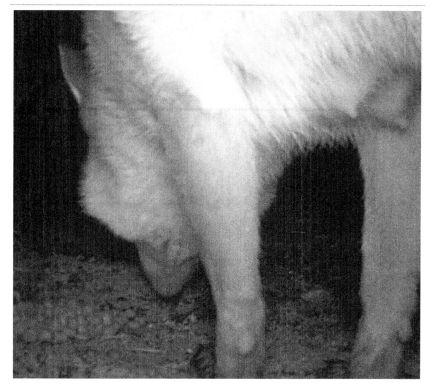

Above: Vix is a nursing vixen.

On 31st March 2020 I posted my first report about Vix on the Self Isolating Bird Club (SIBC):

The vixen visiting my garden is feeding cubs as evidence from the night camera shows. I put out dog food for her every day.

Somewhere there must be cubs. As far as I knew there were no foxes living in any of the neighbouring gardens although I had seen foxes crossing the road. The houses, on the other side of the busy main road, backed onto a large area of public parkland. I found myself worried for the vixen I had come to know. I hoped she was careful on the road and that her cubs were safe. Her den might be under a garden shed or somewhere in the undergrowth. Sadly, not everyone is as happy to see foxes or tolerate them in their garden. I had no idea how old her cubs were I just hoped they were safe.

APRIL 2020

The Fox year- April

This is the month the cubs are most likely to leave the den for the first time. It is in April that you may first notice cubs playing in your garden or fields as they explore the world around them. The vixen will be hunting for herself although the dog fox will still be nearby keeping an eye on the cubs.

The wind blew the magnolia petals and they drifted down to cover the garden in pink confetti. After the daffodils, the tulips appeared and soon pinks, reds and peach colours filled the flowerpots. The buds on the apple tree and pear tree began to form and tiny leaves burst forth. The yellow forsythia flowers were joined by newly emerged green leaves. Blousy red flowers opened on the camelia and rose buds began to swell. Shoots and sprouts were popping up and opening throughout the garden heralding the change in the weather but as a gardener I was aware there was still the possibility of a late frost, a harbinger of doom for any less than hardy bud. There have been years when the apple blossom was killed off by a frost, so nothing was ever guaranteed. A few strong winds could quickly devastate the magnolia's blossoms, so it was best to enjoy them all for as long as they lasted. Nature had a way of reminding us yet again to live in the moment and enjoy the 'now'.

The fact that Vix was out looking for food for herself when clearly nursing made me wonder if she had any help at all raising her cubs. I had seen no other foxes in the garden during the day, so doubted she had a dog fox taking her food. Her coat was not the gorgeous red I associated with a British red fox. She had patches of grey in her scruffy fur and her tail was thin without the characteristic glorious brush. I assumed this was perfectly normal for the time of year as I knew foxes went through a moult but in the back of my mind I wondered if it could be mange. A few years ago, a young fox had been seen in the area with a bad case of mange and had sadly died. It was an awful thing to witness such suffering and it broke my heart but sadly there was nothing I could do to help as the fox disappeared from my garden and was not seen again until its body was found under a neighbour's shed. I hoped Vix was not suffering from the disease and that she was just showing the bedraggled signs of a being a busy nursing mother; the last thing on her mind being her appearance.

Above: Vix with varying colours in her coat.

My house was full of my husband's possessions and I could not face sorting through them, so I took the opportunity of more time at home to sort out the small shedlette at the bottom of my garden. Like many gardeners I had more flowerpots than I could ever need, ties, tags, seed packets, garden stakes and numerous 'useful' bits of wood. My shedlette needed a good de-clutter. I spread its contents around me braving the spiders I had disturbed. Having discovered a long-forgotten box of seeds I sat down in a garden chair and started to rummage through it. I was soon planting seeds, while the chaos of the emptied shed lay momentarily forgotten all around me. It was as I was filling flowerpots with compost that I heard a clatter on the fence that divided my garden from my neighbours. I was used to the sound of the local cats clambering onto the fence, taking a moment to see what I was up to, before deciding to enter the garden, but this was different, the sound suggested something a little heavier. Intrigued, I looked up to see Vix was in the garden strolling backwards and forwards behind the pea plants. She spotted me watching her and froze.

I spoke quietly, keeping my voice calm, my manner matter of fact, as though having a fox in the garden was an everyday occurrence, which at that time it was. I was not bothered at all, no big deal, it was just a fox not more than four metres away from me. In truth I had to contain my excitement so as not to scare her off.

"Hello, there," I said giving her a quick glance before returning my gaze to the flowerpots. I knew enough not to make eye contact for too long. Cats do not like that either. "I'm planting a few seeds," I informed Vix. "I'd be grateful if you did not dig them up."

Vix plodded down the garden to stand further away but continued to watch me, assessing if I was friend or foe. Were my intentions good or bad and what the heck was I waffling on about? It suddenly occurred to me that she may have come to see what was in the food dish at the bottom of the garden; the part of the garden now covered in the contents of the shed. There was some left-over cat food in the dish, but she could not get to it because a pesky woman was in the garden and had placed all sorts of obstacles in the way. I stopped messing about with the seeds and stood up slowly. Vix watched. I walked towards the house and Vix clambered through the flowers moving parallel to me but all the time keeping me a certain safe distance away. It was a strange dance.

"I'll see what I've got to eat that you might like," I told her and went into the house. Mew and Jem greeted me and I explained that I was just getting some food, yes some of their food, to give to the fox. I do not think they were terribly impressed that their pouches of tuna and salmon were about to be given to a 'dog'.

When I returned to the garden with a pouch of cat food, I was delighted to find Vix still there. She hid beneath the small apple tree as I placed the food on the ground beneath the bird feeders and retreated to the metal bench that sat against the wall of the house. I was far enough away to offer no immediate danger but close enough to see what she would do. Vix was rightly suspicious of the food I offered, and she approached slowly before giving it a good sniff, but her hunger got the better of her and she gobbled it down. I sat on the bench with a silly smile on my face and a feeling of warmth running through me. I had done a nice thing for a wild animal, and it felt good. Once the food was gone Vix climbed over the fence and disappeared into my neighbour's garden. That feeling of delight stayed with me for the rest of the day.

I posted about my experience on the Self Isolating Bird Club. Some members were thrilled and excited, but others warned me not to feed foxes as they cause damage when digging up the garden. I am a keen gardener but if Vix decided to dig so be it. I was excited to see her and would happily put up with a bit of digging. Being able to watch a wild fox far outweighed the pleasure a few tiny homegrown strawberries might bring. It was a matter of priorities. Having Vix in my garden was a pleasure. Others said feeding foxes would domesticate them. I had no intention of trying to domesticate Vix, I was just giving food to another living creature who was clearly very hungry and struggling to survive. I had helped a nursing mother before when I looked after Mew. I was happy to help Vix now. However, being a responsible person, I decided it was prudent to research the effects of feeding foxes.

Above: Vix visits when I am in the garden.

A couple of days later, as I worked in the garden, I could hear cars speeding up and down the road at the front of the house and envisaged boy-racers treating the now virtually empty streets as their own personal racetrack. When I took a break and sat sipping a well-deserved cup of tea, I imagined a small fox peering out from between the cars and trying to navigate safely from one side of the road to the other. Then I heard sirens. The police appeared to be giving chase. It was not safe for a mother fox and I was not surprised at how quickly I had grown to care about Vix. All she had to do was stay in my garden whilst I was there, and I was hooked. The new life I had tried to create since Brian's death was now on hold along with the lives of everyone else in the UK. I had a house full of memories and a broken heart. The arrival of a fox had given me something new and wonderful to focus on.

Above: Vix caught in the evening sunlight

As I continued to be blessed by visits from Vix, I made sure I had my camera in the garden whenever I was out there. When Vix licked her lips, I was able to get a good look at her teeth and noticed how healthy and clean they were, despite the condition of her coat. As a wild carnivore, Vix's teeth enamel would not suffer the onslaught of sugar and tea stains my own had to endure. With strong teeth she would have no trouble crunching on bones or ripping flesh from her prey. Those teeth also had the potential to give a nasty bite. However, despite the occasional sensationalist headline, bites from foxes are extremely rare in the United Kingdom. Urban foxes are, in the most part, gentle creatures more likely to run away from your cat than stand and face it. They are generally shy, and most people will only see them from a distance as they go padding down the street in the early morning or late at night. It often transpires that a person who states they were bitten by a fox was trying to feed it by hand and somehow startled it or else they had cornered it causing the scared fox to defend itself in the only way it knew how. Fortunately, dogs and foxes in the United Kingdom do not have rabies so there was no danger of catching that.

Above: Vix shows off her clean teeth

As I taught and prepared work for my students via Skype it was inevitable that I would cast a glance out of the window to my garden. Was Vix out there? I found myself looking out more and more hoping to see my friendly fox. When work on the computer was done, I retreated into the garden to rest my eyes from the screen and to unwind. We were blessed with beautiful warm, sunny weather that spring and it felt good to be outside in the fresh air and to enjoy the calm that had descended on the natural world.

Woody and Wendolyn, the wood pigeons were courting on the back fence. They walked backwards and forwards, touching beaks, fluffing up their feathers and grooming each other. I looked away to give them their privacy as they cemented their bond, although, having chosen the tallest fence on which to consummate their relationship, clearly, they were not at all shy.

I was now regularly placing dog food for Vix below the birdfeeders and occasionally at the edge of my small pond. It became part of her circuit of my garden to sniff under the bird feeder to see what might be available before proceeding to the pond. As I sat on my garden seat, near the house, feeding Hunter, the unpredictable tabby cat, Vix turned up. I watched her out of the corner of my eye not wanting to spook her and turned on my video camera. Hunter headed off to taunt the local sparrows as Vix sniffed at the food by the pond and then came towards me, her eyes on the cat food I had placed on the ground for Hunter. Usually the two neighbourhood carrion crows, Russell and Jo, would gather up any uneaten cat food. Murgatroyd and Maggie, the magpies, always washed the food in the bird bath or fountain before eating it. Now a fox was edging ever closer for the same food. I spoke soothingly to Vix, at least what I hoped was soothing to a fox. She eyed me nervously, her soft brown eyes watching for any sudden move I might make. My heart melted. She was so desperate for food that she was risking her own safety and that of her cubs, because if anything happened to her, they would surely perish. Despite the possible danger the lure of the food was too great and she came ever closer. I remained perfectly still as she ate. She took a few hesitant steps back and then came forward for another mouthful. Vix ate quickly, keeping an eye on me as she did. Finally, she decided it was safe to stay to eat it all. It was incredibly humbling to see a wild animal come that close and to know that she trusted me enough to risk eating the food I had offered. Somehow, I had conveyed to her that I was not a threat, that I would let her eat in peace and without hurting her. To have communicated with a member of another species simply by body language was remarkable.

Above: The closer Vix had ever been to me, so far.

Despite the food I was providing, Vix was looking thinner, her coat greyer, and her tail even more stick-like. Was this due to mange or just the result of her nursing cubs? Members of the SIBC thought it was mange and informed me that many wildlife and fox charities provide free mange treatment. Mange, or sarcoptic mange to give it its proper name, is caused by the mite *Sarcoptes scabiei*. Mites are small arthropods belonging to the Arachnida, the same class as spiders and being parasitic they feed on a host. The mite burrows under the skin of the infected animal and secondary infections can set in as the host scratches and bites at their itching skin. Mange is contagious so if Vix had it she was highly likely to pass it on to her cubs. If a fox is moulting, you can see the new fur underneath. With mange you will see bald patches which tend to start at the back end of the fox and work its way forward as the fox scratches and aids the mites progress through their fur. As Vix's tail was the most obviously affected part it seemed mange was the most likely culprit.

The National Fox Welfare Society and The Fox Project websites both recommended a homeopathic treatment. I am not a believer in homeopathy. I do not understand how adding a few drops of something to a solution, making it so dilute as to be ineffective, can cure you and the placebo effect often attributed to the effectiveness of homeopathy in humans can surely not work on animals. However, it seemed that despite this there were many reported cases of the treated fox getting better. I did wonder if that was simply due to the regular supply of food the concerned human had provided, but, as it would not harm other wildlife should they eat the food containing it, it was worth giving it a go. There was no need to contact a vet and was also something I could send away for on Amazon. It seemed worth a try. I sent for 15 ml of Sulphur 30c, Homeopathic drops for dogs and cats.

When the Sulphur 30c arrived, it was in a small, brown, glass bottle with a dropper. I added drops to the dog food as instructed and watched from the window when Vix appeared. Vix gave the food a sniff and did not eat it. She wandered around the garden and then came back for another look at what was on offer. She ate some but not all of it. Did that mean she could smell something had been added to her food? Had she consumed enough of the sulphur 30c in the small amount she had eaten? Either way it was a start and better than doing nothing. I continued to add the drops to the food I gave her, twice daily.

Above: Vix eating beside the pond.

Above: Vix quickly became easy to recognise.

Above: Vix drinks at the pond

As April continued, white bell-shaped flowers soon hung in clusters on the blueberry bush and the first purple hews were visible at the end of the newly formed lavender flowers. Yellow alyssum and purple campanulas spread across the ground attracting low flying pollinators often moving too fast for me to identify. I threw the drying red camelia flowers into the pond where they floated, like water lilies, adding colour to the garden before sinking to the bottom to provide food for the decomposers. I had planted some wall flowers, as a memory of those my mother used to grow. Their velvet cruciferous flowers filled our garden in the 1970s and appear to have gone out of fashion, but they are reliable bloomers and attract insects. Now the burgundy flowers were buzzing with flying insects once more.

Whenever I sat in the garden, I kept a lookout for Vix and awaited the clatter of paws on the low fence. She would perch there for a moment, checking to see if it were safe to enter and if there was a cat to be avoided. When Vix was happy that all was well, she would land, almost silently, on her two front paws and proceed to patrol the garden giving everything a good sniff as she did so. She might have a drink at the pond, reclaim something previously buried or just sit for a moment in one of the areas of bark chippings. If she were unsure, she would hide behind the plants eyeing me through a break in the leaves. I talked to her as I went about my garden tasks so that she would become familiar with the sound of my voice and hoped the soft tone I used would convey that I meant no harm. I had done nothing to convince her otherwise, but trust was not something a wild animal could afford to give easily.

SIBC members began to recommend food I could provide for Vix. Dog biscuits and raw food were recommended. Could you give foxes the same food as dogs? Were there things I should avoid? Thank goodness for the internet. Years ago, I would have had to wait for the library to open or try to sneak a look through an appropriate book on the shelves in WH Smith. Now, as long as the Wi-Fi was working, with a few clicks I had access to a wealth of knowledge from around the globe and it was interesting to see the different attitudes to foxes in different countries. Some treat them as pets, some as vermin, others an upsetting source of fur. They are merely a commodity with no need of love or compassion. Feed it, grow it, kill it for its fur, repeat. I hate to think about the emotional and physical trauma those poor animals go through.

Many websites mentioned that foxes were more like cats than dogs in their habits. Their adaptability, in an ever-changing human world, has made them remarkably successful. Foxes are most active at night like non-domestic cats and hunt alone by stealth instead of in a pack. Their whiskers are long and sensitive like cats too. Food wise, foxes hunt rabbits and rodents, will eat carrion and earthworms as well as berries and fruit. It seemed the food I had been offering Vix was more than suitable.

OMG Vix this is close.

The sun warmed me as I worked in the garden. We had an incredibly unprecedented hot, dry spell in Spring. It was as if nature recognised we were struggling and gave us the ability to recuperate outdoors. The warm weather continued, and the sky, free of clouds and the contrails of aeroplanes, appeared bluer than I had ever seen it. Silent of man-made objects, the sky was broken only by the occasional fluffy white cloud and the air was filled with the songs of birds. Nature was reclaiming the Earth and it felt good. It was as if the world had been given a chance to recover, to regain what man had taken from it, to be reborn. In the distance I could hear a lawnmower and the buzz of a strimmer as neighbours tidied up their gardens, but I piled cut twigs on the log pile and planned where to scatter wildflower seeds in the hope of making my garden more welcoming to wildlife.

When I sat down to take a breather, I was soon making plans for the garden. Which plants had survived the winter to flower again and which ones needed replacing? As I was pondering Vix appeared. I had placed some food for her to eat on the paving stones beside the pond, but this time she came closer than ever before to see if there is anything else on offer, something the cats had rejected perhaps. I stayed perfectly still not wanting to scare her but also, if truth be told, because I do not know what this wild animal would do and if I was in any danger. The answer was no. Vix just came closer for a sniff to satisfy her curiosity; closer than she had ever been, and I was thrilled once more by her growing trust in me.

MAY 2020

The Fox year- May

The vixen will now be weaning the cubs off her milk. She is likely to rest away from them during the day, returning to the den to provide her cubs with food. Sometimes cubs are spotted out on their own, but this does not mean they have been abandoned, as is often reported to animal welfare groups, they are just exploring around the den site.

The sun moved higher in the sky, bringing to life the solar fountain which began to bubble, filling the garden with the sound of trickling water. The breeze blew the wooden windchimes creating a soothing hollow clanking sound as they bumped into each other. The metal chimes tinkled a gentle accompaniment.

I had bought and painted four hanging baskets and had just finished potting them up with trailing geraniums and lobelia when there was a clatter on the fence and Vix appeared.

"Hello, sweetheart," I said as she did her circuit of the garden.

Although much of her fur was still looking grey, her coat patchy and her tail stick thin, I convinced myself I could see a slight improvement, but in truth she was not looking good.

Above: Vix gives my crocs a sniff

I sat quietly trying not to disturb her as she ate the food beside the pond but once finished, she padded towards me determined to investigate me further. Vix came closer and I did not move, I did not want to startle her, and then she sniffed my pink Crocs. For a moment I thought she was going to grab at them, as I had read about foxes taking gardening gloves and shoes to play with and people discovering an assortment of footwear under their shed or behind the bins. I envisaged myself hopping down the garden trying to wrestle the Croc from between her jaws, but it was only a sniff of curiosity she wanted and not some innate desire to own a pair of pink rubber shoes.

Vix was so thin that I could see the outline of her ribs as she breathed, and I hoped the food I gave her would show results soon. SIBC members were cheering me on in my efforts to help her and their comments were a real boost to my ego and who doesn't need a bit of ego boosting now and then. Others did not think she looked so good, and several people suggested I give her some raw chicken. Members of the SIBC suggested I contact the South Essex Wildlife Hospital for advice.

As I was also having doubts about the effectiveness of the Sulphur 30c I telephoned the wildlife hospital. I spoke to a nice lady who was able to see the photos of Vix on the SIBC Facebook page. She diagnosed mange and said she would show the photos to the vet just to be sure. If the vet agreed it was sarcoptic mange they would send me some medication through the post, but I had to be sure that only the fox to be treated would receive it. Could I do that? Yes, I assured them, I could. The medication would be contained in honey and in preparation for its arrival it was recommended that I give Vix some honey mixed with chicken soup. If she would eat that we knew she would take the medication.

I wanted to do more to help her before the mange treatment arrived and the easiest way was to improve her diet. On my next visit to the supermarket, I found myself adding three fresh chickens to my trolley. One for me to cook for myself and two for a fox. The words 'fox food' along with 'cat food' were now regularly appearing on my shopping list. It was doing wonders for the number of Nectar points I was earning too.

Above: Vix, clearly still nursing, sits in the sunshine.

Above: The portrait of Vix

To see if Vix would take the medicine I was expecting, the next time I saw her I put out a plate containing honey mixed with cold chicken soup. Vix gave it a suspicious sniff. This was not the usual food I offered. She licked it, cautiously, and then literally lapped it all up. I was relieved and it gave me hope that I would be able to help my foxy friend and get rid of the mange.

A couple of days later a package arrived and I opened it to find two small plastic vials containing honey with Panomec, a version of Ivermectin which is used to treat parasitic infestations, mixed in with it. I was to give the contents of the vials to Vix one week apart, hidden in food. I tilted the vial, expecting it to be runny honey. It did not move. Hmm. This might be a problem. How to get the honey out of the vial? The vial was too small for a spoon to fit in being no more than half a centimetre in diameter. There followed a lot of rummaging in the kitchen drawer. You know the one I mean; many households have one. It has lots of 'useful' things in it; a bulldog clip, bits of string, a key to something but you are not sure what so best not to throw it away, a piece of chalk, Post Office rubber bands, a paperclip, a screwdriver, hammer, picture hook, batteries and, at the bottom, found after stabbing my finger on a rogue drawing pin, lolly sticks. With a bit of adapting a lolly stick proved to be just the right size to fit into the small diameter of the medicine vial. I was able to scoop out the honey and mix it with the gravy from some chicken dog food. Now all I needed was a hungry, unsuspecting, and cooperative fox.

Later that afternoon when Vix arrived I knew this was my chance. Trying not to do anything to make Vix suspicious I placed the medicated honey and chicken flavoured mixture beside the pond.

"I've got some chicken flavoured gravy for you," I said as nonchalantly as I could, feigned innocence dripping from every word. "I thought you might like it with a bit of honey in it. Something a little sweet for a change."

Vix listened. Could she detect anything in my voice that would alert her to my cunning plan? This was hardly the double-blind trail I taught my students about. I moved away and sat down trying to convey the air of a casual observer. "See what you think," I suggested casually.

Vix approached the food and gave it a sniff. Would she detect the medication? Would that sensitive nose, capable of identifying other members of her species simply by the scent used to mark their territories, be able to detect even the smallest amount of hidden chemicals in food? If it did, it clearly did not bother Vix because she lapped away at the chicken flavoured gravy and the medicine was delivered to the unsuspecting patient. Sitting nearby, in my flowery wellies, I smiled knowingly. Round one was a success and hopefully Vix's health would start to improve with even the smallest amount of Panomec inside her.

As a treat I gave Vix a large piece of chicken assuming she would take it away to consume at her leisure. Instead, she stayed in the garden and chewed off a piece before crushing the bones with her strong molar teeth and swallowing large chunks whole. The video I posted on Facebook showed Vix eating the raw chicken. There followed a discussion about the merits of giving raw as opposed to cooked meat to dogs, cats and foxes. In raw chicken the bones are cartilaginous and easy for a dog or fox to chew. It is what they would normally feed on if they caught a bird or rat in the wild. Once cooked the bird's bones become brittle and are more likely to splinter and are therefore more dangerous if eaten. It is safer to give animals raw food. We were all learning something thanks to Vix.

Above: Vix enjoys a crunchy treat.

Members of the SIBC were also beginning to study Vix more closely, noticing different things about her coat, her scar and how she looked at me when I spoke to her or she waited for food. There were subtle tilts of her head, the squinting of her eyes and what appeared to be the occasional smile. Vix was becoming a 'personality' and not just another fox.

Above: Vix by the pond. Note her thin tail.

Vix developed a routine of eating a little of the food I gave her before disappearing over the fence with the rest, presumably taking it back to her cubs. Foxes feed their young solely on milk for four weeks, after that, although the cubs will continue to suckle, they start eating solid food too. The vixen will regurgitate food for them. That meant that sometime around the end of April Vix's cubs were eating solid food. They were now at least six weeks old by my reckoning, so the food Vix was taking back was most likely for her young. How many nutrients Vix herself was managing to obtain concerned me. If she was taking food back, suckling the cubs and regurgitating what she had eaten, it was no wonder she was so thin and hungry.

I continued working my way through a list of garden tasks. I split open bags of bark chippings and refreshed the areas around the garden where bare patches had appeared. My efforts were greatly appreciated by the cats and foxes as it gave them something new to rearrange after dark. In the pond the long blades of the water iris began to head skywards and the vertical leaves cast interesting shadows on each other as the sun moved across the sky. I scooped out a mass of blanketweed and left it piled on a paving stone at the edge of the water to allow any water louse, shrimp, or pond snail the chance to make their way back home. After drying for a day or two the weed was placed in the compost bin. The silver birch tree, one of the free trees given away by the Mayor of London, had grown from a stick that dropped through my letter box, to a six-foot-high beauty. By May its leaves unfurled, and the thin trunk swayed in the breeze.

A few days later Vix decided to rest up in my garden. She rested her chin on her stretched out front paws, with her back legs extended behind her, assuming what I could only think to call, the downward dog position. It was a position she adopted many times and I wondered if it was more comfortable for a nursing mother to lay like that. Whatever the reason, it must have suited Vix because she was soon fast asleep. It was humbling to see a wild animal, which I had to remind myself Vix still was, feel so secure in my presence that she could close her eyes and sleep close to me. SIBC members loved seeing her so relaxed. This was not the cunning fox we were so often shown in cartoons nor an evil killer that needed chasing. This was an exhausted mother who had found a safe place to rest and I was happy to let her do so.

Above: Vix assumes her downward dog position

Despite the threat of coronavirus, I was enjoying my time at home. The weather was wonderful allowing me to spend time in the garden where I felt more relaxed. Indoors, I was still surrounded by my husband's possessions which at some point I had to sort out. Every box reminded me that he was gone. Every jacket hanging on a door reminded me of our life together and if I brushed close enough, I could still smell his presence in the fabric. I would often press my face into the material and breathe in his familiar smell, taking a moment just to remember him. As I passed by, I would lay a hand on a piece of his clothing and pause before giving it a pat and moving on. If you have never watched a loved one fade and die you will never know the heartache. The overwhelming sadness of it all. I have done it twice and it is brutal.

Sorting through Brian's things had become all about 'getting rid of'; as if I was trying to remove all evidence of him from the planet and that hurt. Photographs of Brian's family, uncles, aunts, parents and grandparents, I put aside to pass on to his sister and nephew. Receipts, bank statements and bills kept the shredder whirring away on many days. I wanted to keep the books that I knew meant something to Brian. His collection of

Julian Barnes and Alexander Kent novels I put in a box alongside biographies of Tour de France rider Miguel Indurain, and Star Trek stars Leonard Nimoy and James Doohan.

The boxes, bags and suitcases reminded me of the man I had lost and the life I no longer had. At times, the grief became unbearable. Often when I was doing the washing-up; my mind would wander, and the enormity of my loss would overwhelm me, and I would sink to the kitchen floor and sob my heart out. A good cry was cathartic, releasing the tension that had built up over the preceding days of sorting. At other times just getting through the day itself was the hardest thing to do. The amount of 'stuff' in my house was overwhelming. I felt like a hoarder and could understand why they never tackle the piles and piles around them. Where do you start? Everything contained a memory. Everything reminded me of the 'never more'. And with charity shops closed what did you do with it all? And how could I throw away the things that had been important to him, that had meant so much to him? I knew from experience that it would take time. I would get there in the end but the journey to 'getting there' hurt so much.

Indoors, despite the best efforts of Mew and Jem, there were painful memories. There was the sofa Brian sat on as I covered him with a blanket to keep him warm, and the bed he slept in for days on end when his strength failed. The room he slept in was the dying room. I had hung photographs of Brian's Mum, Dad, Sister and Aunt, on the wall so that he could see the people he loved and be reminded of happier times as he lay there knowing his own days were numbered. It was the end of all things for Brian. The thought of that still fills me with overwhelming sadness and sucks the energy from my core. How do you face your own approaching death? Was it a relief to Brian, to know that the pain would soon be over? Did he feel life had lost all reason? I will never know the answers.

Brian has been gone long enough. I miss him, he can come back now...but he never will. Memories of our time together are full of heartache for what will never be again. They remind me he is no longer here. Hopefully, a time will come when the memories bring a smile but having cared for my Mum and Brian, I know that the most recent memories of them are not ones I want to relive and even my wedding photo feels me with heartache, reminding me of what was to come.

Out in the garden there was bird song, the sound of children bouncing on a trampoline and the occasional visiting fox. Outside there were no boxes of memories to sort through, no constant reminders of all I had lost. Outside everything was new and life continued. With a cat screen over the open French doors even Mew and Jem could be with me as I sat in the open air and let nature soothe me.

I had also taken to painting flowerpots. I was trying to create a Moroccan feel to a small area of the garden where I had placed Brian's potted palms and could not find a blue flowerpot in the shade I wanted. I had a light bulb moment and the idea of painting my own developed. The appropriate colour paint was just a click away on Amazon and once it arrived, I spent many a happy hour coating terracotta pots in Ultramarine blue before adorning them with my own unique designs using acrylic pens. I began with flowers, tried mandala-style patterns, and moved on to my own cartoonish designs. I was not an artist but enjoyed releasing my creative side and am told it is considered folk art. I'm happy to call it that.

One afternoon as I painted, Vix appeared and wandered around the pots, having a good sniff as she did so. I was worried she would get paint on her fur and become known as the blue fox, but she was careful, maybe the smell put her off getting too close. However, she did appear interested in my camera, possibly seeing her own reflection in the glass of the lens. Keeping an eye on it she moved closer. I stayed perfectly still so as not to startle her, and she sniffed the lens or maybe the fox she could see reflected there. I was within fox breathing distance and looked into those beautiful brown eyes.

Above: Vix comes so close.

During another flowerpot painting session, I laid a piece of black pond liner on the ground to sit on as I worked and to stand the pots on later as they dried. I went indoors to wash the brushes and returned to find Vix taking advantage of a dark material's ability to absorb and emit infrared radiation. Well, maybe she did not know about the infrared, but it was obviously nice and warm under paw. I grabbed my camera to take a quick photo and after a few moments she noticed what I was doing. Vix sat up, then arched her back as she stood up and stretched. She looked directly at me and the camera I insisted on holding all the time and poked out her tongue. It may be overt anthropomorphism, but I think Vix was having a laugh.

Above: Vix relaxes on my painting mat

Above: Vix pokes her tongue out at me.

Later that afternoon Vix returned, from what I assumed was a trip back to the cubs, and settled down in the shade, on a cool patch of concrete, on what some may generously call my patio. I sat nearby reading and spoke gently to her as I did so. She was clearly exhausted as she had trouble keeping her eyes open. I watched as she finally gave in to exhaustion, closed her eyes and let sleep take her. Her breathing steadied as she snoozed. I sat quietly reading letting her sleep, once again humbled that she would place herself in such a vulnerable position and yet trust me to do her no harm. If I could give this little fox somewhere to sleep I would do so. If my presence made her feel safe then I would stand guard. How could I not be totally enamoured by her? Vix shifted position, stretching out her legs, as the tension left her body and she relaxed. I turned the pages of my book quietly, aware that she was still alert to any sound that might mean danger. To live on your wits must be exhausting.

Above: Vix finds a quiet place to rest

SIBC members encouraged me to keep posting about Vix, they had taken her to their hearts, and many had started to look for my posts about her. It was nice to feel cared about again. Some people, many living in rural areas and not so used to seeing foxes as I was, were surprised that a wild animal could be so trusting or that a fox would be seen during the day. I was told I must have an 'aura' about me for Vix to feel safe in my presence, which to me suggested I did not smell too bad. It never occurred to me that what I was doing was special. I had just seen another living being struggling and had offered help. My ego was given a huge boost by the comments people posted but at no time was that my motivation. I wanted to help Vix and if seeing what I was doing and following her story gave others pleasure then that made me happy too. I would have done exactly the same with or without the Facebook following. Perhaps, others in turn would be encouraged to help a fox they knew and in this way, the happiness I felt, and a greater appreciation of foxes, would spread and a few more vulnerable lives would be saved.

In a time of great anxiety, when many people were self-isolating, seeing no one for days on end and staring at their own four walls, the plight of a small nursing vixen had captured their imagination. It was completely understandable to me. You only had to look at that gorgeous foxy face and those big brown eyes to be captivated. How could you not fall in love with her? Vix was certainly helping me through isolation. I looked forward to her visits, although Mew and Jem were not so keen, and I am sure, on more than one occasion, I saw them glaring at her through the cat-screen, that covered the open door.

The images I painted on my flowerpots were of things that meant something to me. I painted sunflowers because I had often grown them in my garden; Monarch butterflies reminded me of all the times I had seen them in Canada, fluttering in the air as if pulled by the strings of an invisible puppeteer. The turtles I painted were for my husband who saw them as his spirit animal, and they reminded me of the green turtle we watched swimming in the Indian Ocean on our trip to the Seychelles. For as long as I can remember I have drawn a palm tree on a beach as a doodle, so that had to be on a flowerpot. I drew cats to represent Mew, Jem, Tux and Hunter and it was only a matter of time before I painted a tribute to Vix on a pot. I Googled how to draw foxes and I think Vix was secretly pleased with the result. She even obliged me by posing with a pot.

Above: Vix poses with my blue pot portrait of her

I was concerned that Vix would attempt to taste or drink the paint brush cleaner I had poured into an empty dog food tin and placed on the bench beside me as I worked, but Vix was smarter than that. However, she clearly failed to grasp the new concept of social distancing as she worked her way under the bench I was sitting on so that she could sniff me.

Above: Vix failing to understand social distancing

15th May 2020

Vix had shown a liking for the gravy that came with the chicken and vegetable dog food I put out for her, so when it came time to give Vix her second dose of Panomec mange treatment I mixed it in with chicken gravy. Once again, Vix gave the food a sniff and I stood back hoping she would not detect what lay within. If she did, it clearly did not matter because Vix ate it all. Her mange treatment was now complete, and I hoped we would soon see an improvement in her coat and overall condition.

Above: Vix consumes the second dose of medication (video capture)

When the topic of whether it was advisable to feed foxes was raised once more on Facebook, it seemed the main fear many people had was that the foxes would become dependent on whoever feeds them and not hunt or search for food themselves. What would happen if the feeder was no longer able, or willing, to provide food? Would the fox starve? Would they approach other people with disastrous consequences? There is also talk of falsely increasing the carrying capacity of the environment by providing food but, I consider it readdressing the balance.

Foxes are perfectly capable of finding food for themselves and if they are not overfed, they will not become dependent on you. Many foxes live in areas we have constructed homes on and perhaps, having destroyed their natural habitat, this obligates us to help. I looked upon it as supplementing Vix's diet and reducing the time she needed to spend away from her cubs, rather than providing all the food she needed.

Another worry was that foxes would lose their fear of humans and approach everyone, causing people to misinterpret the approach as a threat. What if the fox accidentally, or even deliberately, bit you?

Foxes, just like a pet dog or cat, can tell people apart. Just because one person feeds them does not mean they will lose their natural caution around others and approach anybody. I had seen Vix move nervously away from people in the street even after spending time with me in the garden. I had no worries for her on that score.

The fox/human relationship was a discussion that would run throughout my SIBC posts about Vix, and discussion is a good thing, something to encourage. Through debate we may learn something new, educate ourselves and others and perhaps even changed someone's point of view and save another fox's life.

Above: Vix settles down for a nap

As if aware of the controversy surrounding feeding her, Vix pulled out all the stops to look extra adorable the next day. It was another warm afternoon, she had eaten the chicken I provided, and I spotted her through the window, snoozing near a flowerbed. I love that she considered my garden a haven; a safe place where she could sleep peacefully and recharge her foxy batteries. Her nipples were clearly visible, although only the back ones were prominent, which suggested she was feeding just two or three cubs. She looked so relaxed and content that I decided not to go outside as I did not want to disturb her. I watched through the window as her side rhythmically rose and fell with her breathing. As I look at this photograph again, I still see a smile of contentment on her face. She really was the most adorable fox.

Only two days after Vix had the second dose of mange treatment I thought I saw an improvement in her coat. It may have been the light or the angle that I saw her from, or wishful thinking on my part, but I was convinced her coat looked thicker and healthier. Once again with hindsight she still had a lot of improving to do.

Above: Vix's thin tail is clearly visible as she eats.

Above: Vix at her adorable best

Sometimes I was so busy videoing or photographing Vix or sorting out which food to give her that I forgot to just be with her; to share a moment, and to watch. She would give me such a trusting look, her eyes meeting mine and I often wrinkled my nose in return. She had such soulful eyes, and I felt a deep connection to her as I chatted away, convinced she understood my intentions if not the precise meaning of my words. She sat close to me, waited patiently as I prepared what to feed her and ate and slept in my presence. It is an understatement to say I felt humbled. I loved every minute of it. Each time was special and unique. Vix did not have to visit, she did not have to trust me, but she did and how could that not be anything but wonderful.

On one of the many glorious sunny days we had during lockdown, Vix found a shady spot under the hypericum bush and settled down for a snooze. There is something special about that part of the garden because the stray cats like to sleep there too. It is in the shade and any animal sheltering there will have its back against the garden fence, so no one can creep up on you when you are vulnerable. It was the perfect place for a nap.

I pottered in the garden casting the occasional glance in Vix's direction to see if she was all right. Her fur rose and fell steadily as she snoozed, and all appeared to be well. When she finally stirred, she gave a huge yawn. Fortunately, I had my camera to hand as I was attempting to photograph bees on the purple sage flowers, and I was able to capture her mid-yawn and snapped a photograph of her beautiful white teeth. Red foxes have 42 teeth, ten more than humans. They have 12 incisors, 4 canines, 16 premolars and 10 molars. The first molars are flesh shearing carnassial teeth. Although I could not count all the ones in Vix's mouth, from what I could see they looked healthy with not a visible stain on them. It just goes to show what a diet free of sugar can do for you. When I study that photograph again, I also wonder at the power of the bite those teeth could give and how hard it would be to struggle free once a prey animal was caught.

Above: A Yawning Vix shows off her teeth.

Much to their surprise many people had found that working from home was a possibility they had never conceived of. Before lockdown it sounded like something that would take ages to set up, requiring lots of new and expensive equipment, but when push came to the proverbial shove, we found that technology had moved on and it was simple to do, requiring little more than downloading some software and being adaptable. Most people chose to use Skype or Zoom, and once you had figured out the basics you were ready to go. You could even connect to the world via your phone; how amazed our ancestors would have been by such technology. Of course, I made sure there was nothing in the background of my living room that I did not want my students to see, so a regular check was made for dirty laundry or dishevelled cushions. The occasional visit by Mew or Jem was more than acceptable.

Once, when I was teaching, I spotted Vix in the garden and watched as she found a comfortable position and settled down for another snooze. I wanted desperately to be out there with her, sitting on the bench keeping watch as she slept. However, work had to come first but I was still able to keep an eye on her through the window. As soon as I could be with her, I grabbed an egg and went outside. I meant to give her the egg whole but accidently dropped it and then watched, fascinated to see if, and how, she would eat it. Vix lapped up the egg white first, which was a little gross if you are not a fan of snot-like substances dangling from a mouth, and then she enjoyed the broken yolk. On future visits she preferred the egg to be broken for her and I may have created a diva. I waited to see her lap up the egg white, but she decided she liked the yolk best instead. I could see why foxes are often likened to cats in their habits, unpredictable and a bit fussy, but equally lovely.

Above: Vix snoozes in the garden.

Above: Vix enjoys an egg

Vix developed a regular pattern in her visits and once in the garden she would stay for forty-five minutes or more. Sometimes, if she fell asleep, she might be with me for over an hour. When she failed to turn up at her usual time, I found myself becoming anxious. I was reminded yet again that Vix was visiting me on her terms and there was never a guarantee that she would return. I still had no idea where she went after she had crossed the road. I could only hope that she had somewhere safe to be and that her cubs were also protected when she was not with them. And then the fence would rattle as she jumped over it and she would give me a squinty smile as she sniffed about the garden and all would be well, my fears assuaged. Vix decided to sit for a moment on the spring onions I had planted in my vegetable patch, and I could only hope that they would bounce back up once the weight of a fox was lifted from them. If they were beyond rescue, I did not care because Vix being there meant more to me than a few spring onions.

I may have been helping Vix, but she was helping me too. When she was there, I did not feel so lonely, I felt needed, and she made me feel loved. Mew and Jem did exactly that every day but, as I struggled through my grief, Vix provided a new distraction and a new sense of purpose. Vix showed me there was still a life to be had beyond grief and that new experiences awaited. Since Brian's death I had become acutely aware of my own mortality calculating that if I was lucky, I had twenty years left, assuming they were healthy ones and did not require a carer, as my Mum had. As I sorted through Brian's possessions, I wondered what would happen to my own. At times I could almost hear the clock ticking away the time I had left on Earth; a countdown to my ever-approaching death and demise. Vix brought a fresh interest, a world of learning new things and inexplicable trust that renewed my faith in my own self-worth and value in the years ahead. Vix helped raise my self-esteem and after so much darkness she made me smile. In the same way that Mew helped me heal following my mother's death, Vix was doing the same now that I was a widow. I did not have to explain myself to Vix, I could just be with her, and I needed that more than I realised.

Above: Vix shows how cute she can be

Above: Vix makes eye contact.

Vix had been looking me in the eye on several visits, not in a menacing way but with something akin to curiosity, although some SIBC members informed me it was the look of love. I certainly felt she was smiling and content if that was possible. Dogs and their owners make eye contact all the time and that is vastly different to trying to out-stare a dog, which is not recommended. Vix and I making eye contact felt like a polite acknowledgement between friends, "Hello, how are you, nice to see you again." "I'm fine, thanks. I'm so pleased you are back." "Got any eggs?" I treasured those moments with my smiley friend.

The menu I offered Vix consisted of eggs and raw chicken, or chompy-chicken as I had taken to calling it after watching her chomp away on one piece. Her coat was starting to look better, and dog owners offered advice on foods that would continue to enhance its appearance. Fish oils and omega 3 were suggested and the various foods that might contain them. As always, I did my own research before feeding anything to Vix. I wanted to make sure that what was safe for a cat or dog was also safe for a fox. In the end I bought a tin of sardines in sunflower oil. Yet more food had appeared on my shopping list for a fox. When I placed the sardines on the ground Vix gave them a lick as she did with all food, clearly investigating the smell and flavour before deciding of it was something she would like. She licked up the sunflower oil and then began to devour the sardines. More nutrients were entering her exhausted body. Hopefully, it was another step towards improving her health.

Above: Vix, the day she made contact.

Vix had grown more trusting of me over the weeks, but I never tried to hand feed her, nor deliberately encouraged her closer. She originally came nearer to me because she could not wait for me to sort out the food and decide where to put it. On 24th May as I was placing the food on the ground, I felt a wet nose gently touch my hand. Vix touched me. Deliberately. A little wet 'boop', a nose-bump, and I was ecstatic. It felt like a vindication of her trust in me; an acknowledgement on her part that, "I've been watching you and you seem okay. I trust you now." I was humbled by the very thought. I had been wary when Vix first started to move closer to me and it was not something I had actively encouraged, just her insistence that if the food was there, she was going to wait for it nearby. I was never sure what she would do and as is sensible I remained wary of any animal with sharp teeth. However, as time moved on, I began to feel comfortable in her presence, learning to trust her as she grew to trust me. When she nose-bumped me I was not afraid, because Sasha had taught me, all those years ago, that dogs can be trusted too. And then to top it off Vix sat in a flowerpot, in the sunshine, just to prove how adorable she was.

Above: *Vix Sitting in a flowerpot...as you do.*

Above: Vix snoozes in her favourite spot.

On recent visits, after something to eat, Vix had taken to sleeping beside my small vegetable plot with her head on the bricks I used to create a mini patio for three potted palms to stand on. It was a tiny part of the garden; I pretentiously called my 'Moroccan' area. The palms had been my husband's. I salvaged as many plants as I could from the small garden at Brian's house. Some, like geraniums, bulbs, a couple of the palms and a daphne were already in pots. Others had to be dug up. It took a bit of brute strength to persuade the small apple tree to give up its grip on the ground but the thyme, magnolia, skimmia and euonymus came with me more easily. Leaves and branches waved about in my car as I drove home from Brian's hoping that no spiders would decide to vacate the pots and set up home in my car. One wingmirror spider was enough for me. By bringing the plants back to my house I felt I was bringing a part of Brian too. I did not need things to help me remember him but when I tended the plants or looked at their flowers I hoped, sometime in the future when the pain was not so raw, that they would bring a smile. I talked to Brian, or rather I chatted to his picture, telling him what I was going to plant where or, when out the in garden, I would simply talk out loud assuming that wherever his spirit was, he would hear me. I think he would like the Moroccan area and appreciate Vix choosing to rest there.

For Vix, the Moroccan area was a quiet spot in the shade, with a cool brick pillow, away from prying eyes. I spotted her snoozing when I looked out of the window, and she had that imperceptible smile on her face. If ever I had to choose a name for my home, I would call it The Haven. I have tried to make my garden a haven for all wild creatures. I have butterflies and bee attracting flowers, water dishes, a bird bath, pond, insect houses and several unused bird boxes. So far it has also proved to be a haven for several stray cats. After Mew, two other pregnant females have taken refuge in the plastic cat shelters I have placed around the garden. I arranged for both cats to be collected and taken to animal rescue centres as I knew their kittens were unlikely to survive if born in the wild. Three male cats, Tux, Hunter and Ginge, also know they will be safe from humans, if not other cats, in my garden. As all three are still 'intact', there are the usual territorial disputes which seems to involve the slow movements of cat tai-chi, long staring contests and at times a bit of hissing. Occasionally a full-blown fight will break out when one cat finds himself unexpectedly cornered. It is at that point that I use my teacher's voice on them, which they ignore, although a bit of clapping and the occasional dousing with a splash of water from the watering can seems to send them on their way and awards me a look of feline indignation.

Above: Vix enjoys a rest

Reading is a relaxation for me. Thanks to recommendations by Chris Packham and Megan McCubbin in their online daily SIBC live streams, I had discovered Wild Remedy by Emma Mitchell. Like Emma I suffer from depression and SAD (Seasonally Affected Disorder), although the latter is self-diagnosed. I have always been one to turn on a light when others think it is bright enough in a room. My mood takes a downward direction on grey cloudy days and when we reach the dark days of November, I find my enthusiasm wanes. My husband said, when my November blues took hold, "You always feel this way at this time of year". Brian was right. I am affected by the amount and quality of light I see and more natural light is definitely better. I also find great solace being surrounded by nature. My holidays are never planned in search of nightlife, restaurants, and based on the size of the swimming pool. I do not care if there is a casino, an 'all you can eat' buffet or promises of unlimited alcohol. I want to see the natural landscape and the wildlife wherever I go. When I visited Las Vegas, I was thrilled to learn I could drive to the Grand Canyon from there, the casinos were secondary to my enjoyment of Nevada and Arizona. Whenever I can I want to stand on a beach and gaze out at the ocean as I listen to waves lapping on the shore. I want to scour the water for a sign of a dolphin's fin or the bobbing head of a seal. I want to stand perfectly still once more whilst a deer makes its way down a woodland path ahead of me. I am happiest when there are animals near me, when I can watch them, be with them and perhaps even make that ultimate connection and touch them. The natural world makes me happy and throughout lockdown more and more people began to realise that it does the same for them too.

I was sitting in the garden reading Emma's book, her words resonating with me, when Vix arrived. She appeared curious as to what I was doing. What was the thing I had in my hand that was taking all my attention? Was it edible? Would I offer her some? I placed the book beside me on the bench and, as if to confirm all Emma has written, that nature can indeed heal us, Vix came closer and made me smile as she sniffed the cover of the book. There could not have been a more fitting confirmation of the book's title. Vix was the wild remedy healing me.

Above: Vix giving Emma's book a nose bump of approval?

The warm weather persisted, allowing me to spend more and more time in the garden. Mew and Jem are indoor cats but to give them some access to the sounds and smells that I was enjoying outside I had purchased a cat screen. It was fixed over the opening of the French doors and allowed them to feel the sun on their fur or the wind gently ruffling it. Mew would sit staring out at the world, listening to the twittering of the birds. I am sure she would have loved to go outside and explore, both my garden and those of my neighbours. I felt a twinge of regret that my allergy to cat flea bites meant she was confined, however she seemed happy to sit by the open door, her nose tilted to catch the 'sniffs' carried on the wind. Sometimes Mew becomes agitated by the lure of the open door and I do occasionally take her out for a supervised bit of wandering. I keep an eye on her because I do not want her legging it over the fence or have her come, unexpectedly, face to face with one of the male cats. The short soirees seem to satisfy Mew and she will settle down once back indoors. Seeing how the male cats fought and the way other female cats have been treated I am glad Mew and Jem have been saved from any unwanted attention and the dangers of the cars on the road. As my girls gazed at the garden, Hunter, one of the stray cats, sheltered under a bush or sought the shade of a chair and Vix would pop by for a snooze or bite to eat. A blackbird sitting high on a chimney pot sang out at the end of the day as I sat in the garden my hands cupped around a mug of tea. Despite the horrendous pandemic it was an idyllic time to be outside.

It was no surprise when, having popped indoors to fetch something, I returned to find Vix waiting for me. However, I did not expect to find her sitting in my seat and looking, once more, so utterly adorable. Butter would not melt in this fox's mouth. Fortunately, I was able to take a quick photo. I posted it on Facebook and once again my fox friend won hearts around the world just by being herself. She was an excellent ambassador for her species. Vix was not the cunning, sneaky looking fox of many stories, instead she was a mother with a beautiful smile, expressive eyes and a cheeky personality.

Above: Vix sitting in my place.

Many members of the SIBC commented on the way I spoke to Vix in the videos I posted. They enjoyed our 'conversations' however one sided they might be. Ever since I heard animals 'talk', thanks to the skills of the inimitable Johnny Morris on the 1960s children's television programme Animal Magic, I have also made animals 'talk' or at least put words into their mouths. I do the same with inanimate objects too. Who knew toasters complained so much about being left switched on or televisions wished you would just select a channel and stick to it instead of endlessly scrolling through the menu! Even my kettle has been known to mutter when I asked it to boil some water and then did not use it. Brian found himself also putting words into creatures' mouths after I had given voice to a dog carrying a particularly large stick. He was being urged by his owner to 'Hurry up'. "I can't, can I? I got dis schtick in me mouth", the dog 'replied'. It seemed so obvious to me what the dog was thinking, and I am surprised to find others don't do it too.

Years ago, a female colleague brought her son into school, and he asked if he could see the rats we looked after. One of the rats was brought into the prep room and allowed to wander on the bench. The rat was happy in my hands when I picked it up but was unsure the boy would be able to hold him so securely. "Ooh, I'm going up! Don't let him drop me!" it exclaimed. I assured the rat that I would make sure he was safe, and as he settled down, he gave the boy a good sniff. "He smells funny. Has he had a wash recently?" The boy laughed and I explained that contrary to popular belief, rats are fastidious about personal hygiene and therefore a smelly human would not please them. From then on, her son referred to me as 'the lady that made the rat talk'. To me it seems obvious what other sentient beings are thinking even if they cannot voice those feelings using our language. Anthropomorphising? Of course, I am but how can you be sure I was not actually channelling a rat?

Above: Vix in the sunshine showing off her amazing ears

In May the baby birds arrived. First the sparrow fledglings, their beaks outlined in yellow, fluffed themselves up like tiny tennis balls, and perched on a branch waiting to be fed. Then the squawky starlings followed their parents relentlessly around the garden giving them not a moments peace as they filled the air with their noisy cries. The robins, great tits and blue tits fed their young with more caution and, camera ever at the ready, I waited for their tiny progeny to appear.

Vix proved to be a highly photogenic fox. Her boopable nose, smiley face and huge ears were a hit with the SIBC. She certainly seemed to be a happier fox than when I first met her. Vix's mischievous personality also shone through in the photographs. She had a penchant for climbing over the flowerpots or walking through the plants to get somewhere when the easier route would be to walk past me. She was often seen sticking her nose into a flower to sniff it, burying fat balls in the flowerpots or taking away dog treats and hiding them beneath the bark chippings. However, I think it was the way she would sit, so doglike, in front of me, waiting to see what I was going to do or offer her next, that made her so appealing. She had won my heart and that of a few hundred others.

Despite still being in lockdown, we were allowed to go out for exercise, and I decided to see if I could find out where Vix might live or have her den. It was the first time since lockdown began that I had left my home for something other than to shop for food. I knew the parkland where Vix's den might be located. The houses on the opposite side of the road to me backed onto a field that was also a public space. In recent years areas of wildflowers had been planted and left to grow when the rest of the grass was mown, and a variety of deciduous and coniferous trees provided dappled shade and a glade to walk in. Where the fences of the houses met the field there were patches of bramble, shrubs, and lots of lovely undergrowth for wildlife to feed and build their homes. It was a great place for a fox to rest during the day or hide a litter of cubs. When I arrived, a few people were already taking advantage of the warm sunny day, one sat reading a book, others had brought a picnic, children chased each other, and all were socially distanced. How strange that it had already become the norm to see people sitting themselves a set distance apart. I wandered along the fence armed with my camera. I took photographs of the trees and the light shining through their leaves and branches. I ran my hand over the wonderfully textured bark of a majestic oak. It is always good to look up when you are under trees. The branches seen against the sky are akin to the arteries and veins in our body as they fan out in Fibonacci patterns. There was a beautiful ash tree and I peered skywards to view its canopy of pinnate leaves. In the undergrowth I searched for any sign of foxes such as a well-worn path of flattened grass marking an animal track. I found a few likely places where a fox might be but there was no sign of the resident.

It was as I was lying on the ground photographing a patch of wildflowers that two of my neighbours spotted me. They called out, curious as to what I was up to. I suddenly realised how much I had missed face to face conversation with real three-dimensional people. I had spoken to my brother every day using What's App, chatted to friends on the telephone and to students via Skype but here were actual people. Physical beings to talk to. It was refreshing. My neighbours had decided to take their daily exercise together and it was odd to see them walking together but keeping the recommended two metres apart. We stood spaced out, like the points of an invisible isosceles triangle, and chatted about the crazy situation the world found itself in, how no one could have predicted it and how we were passing the days. When the topic of Vix came up I discovered that a vixen had raised four cubs beneath a shed in a garden not far from me. The cubs had been seen playing in the gardens but were they Vix's cubs or the litter of another vixen? The probability was high that it was her and that meant Vix might still be feeding four cubs. I returned home to await the hungry vixen buoyed by the news that cubs had been seen.

Above: Vix relaxes in the sunshine

Above: Vix gives her squinty smile

Above: Vix relaxes in the shade beside some of the painted flowerpots

JUNE 2020

The Fox year- June

This is the month most people will first see a fox cub. While the vixen is off hunting the cubs stay near the den and play. The vixen will return frequently with food but by the end of the month the cubs are usually weaned off her milk, the den is abandoned, and all of the foxes sleep above ground.

On the first day of June, the weather was warm and sunny. Vix came by as I pottered in the garden and took away several pieces of chompy-chicken. She lapped up the egg, I insisted on breaking to ensure she took some nutrients for herself, instead of giving everything to her cubs. Vix also munched her way through a pouch of dogfood. As I was placing the food on the ground she came nearer. I was no longer worried about what she might do, the trust between us was mutual and when she came closer, I was prepared to feel the bump of a cool wet nose on my hand but instead she licked my knee.

Above: Vix enjoys the shade

Dogs often lick people to show affection. Was it the same for foxes? Was Vix thanking me? Letting me know she liked me? Whatever the reason I was thrilled Vix had made another connection with me. She licked my knee!!! A fox licked my knee!! It was such a simple thing but to me it was massive. I loved her and trusted her and enjoyed every encounter. I sat beaming at her and Vix squinted back.

On Facebook, Vix's followers were growing in number, including many from other parts of the world where foxes were either not so visible or viewed less favourably. It was heart-warming to see that Vix was providing a glimmer of hope in the time of a deadly virus, furlough and social bubbles. Across the United Kingdom hundreds of thousands of employees were on reduced hours and reduced pay with the UK Government topping up their wages. Under the furlough scheme, originally announced by the Chancellor of the Exchequer, Rishi Sunak, employers were able to claim from the government, 80% of the wages paid to an employee. The cost to the UK government would run to billions of pounds. How this would affect government finances and their ability to fund future plans was yet to be seen. With so many forced to stay at home and exist on a reduced income Vix was doing her bit to raise morale.

After all the to-ing a fro-ing with food for her family, and the added responsibility of raising the morale of the nation, Vix settled down, in the Moroccan area, her head resting on the wooden edging, and drifted off for a forty-minute snooze. It was such a special time to share with her although once again, Mew and Jem, watching through the screen, were not so enthusiastic. I tried not to make them jealous of Vix but wonder quite what they thought of the 'dog' in the garden receiving so much of my attention.

Above: Fast asleep in the Moroccan area.

Above: Vix resting where she feels safe.

3rd June 2020

Whilst hanging up my laundry on the washing line, Hunter, one of the stray cats, bit me on the calf. He was always unpredictable, growling and lashing out for no apparent reason or when trying to get my attention. I assumed he had not been properly socialised as a kitten or that his only way to gain attention was to lash out, much like a child who finds they are only noticed by their parents when they scream and shout. I had been working on positive reinforcement to encourage him to choose more desirable behaviour.

"Good boy. Good boy, Hunter," I praised when he did what I wanted. "No!" I would say firmly if he lashed out. We had made some progress but Hunter biting me was new. I felt a sudden pain in my calf and looked down to see him looking back grumpily hoping for some treats. He was not getting any today.

I tended to the wound, washing the two bleeding puncture marks with antiseptic. It was not serious, and the bleeding stopped quickly but all Googled advice said to seek medical attention. I did not want to go to hospital in the middle of a pandemic, but I did not want to suffer any serious infection. I telephoned 111 the NHS helpline and was advised to go to hospital. I drove to the hospital, put on a face mask, and sought out to the Urgent Care department. Fortunately, patients were able to sit and wait a safe distance apart but as I breathed behind the mask my glasses kept steaming up. It made me wonder how doctors and nurses, who wore glasses, coped with the personal protective clothing they were now forced to wear. If I found wearing a mask for just a few minutes uncomfortable and inconvenient, what must it be like to have to wear one all day, every day, whilst being physically active as you try to save lives? I had a better appreciation of all they were enduring. We owe our NHS staff a debt we may never be able to repay. Throughout Brian's treatment for cancer, I made sure to thank the doctors and nurses every time I saw them. The surgeon who saved his life that first night received more than one hug from me and I took baskets of hand cream, smelly candles, and lip balm to every ward Brian was in, as my way to say thank you. I had seen the amount of chocolate they receive and decided against contributing to the threat of diabetes overhanging them. They may have been 'just doing their job' but it never hurts to say thank you to those you know have gone above and beyond.

When my turn at Urgent Care came, the bite wound was assessed, and I was reassured that I had done all the right things as cat bites can be 'nasty' and full of bacteria. The wound was cleaned again, and I was given a tetanus injection before heading on my way. When people started to ask if I was worried about Vix biting me I wanted to say no, I think she is safer than a cat, but I kept that story to myself until now.

Vix had taken to sitting in a particular spot on the concrete patio while she waited for her food. For whatever reason, no matter where I placed the food in the garden, Vix had decided that she would sit near the black storage box, Tux's cat shelter behind her, a row of painted flowerpots beside her whilst she waited for food to be served. And so, it became known as 'her spot'.

Above: Vix waits patiently

I had my camera with me whenever I was in the garden to photograph flowers and birds but also to record my encounters with Vix. She often gave the camera a curious look, unsure what the weird device was or why I seem so obsessed with having it nearby. On one particular day she came close and booped the camera with her nose, smudging the lens. And then we made eye contact. We were always looking at each other but something more passed between us in that intense look. It was a remarkable moment of shared trust between members of two different species. I spoke to her, my voice barely more than a whisper, but I cannot remember a word I said, just that I felt overwhelming love and deep understanding. It was as if she was acknowledging our friendship.

Above: Vix up close and personal

A day or so later Vix and Hunter were in the garden, Vix waiting in her spot and Hunter munching on a handful of cat treats I had placed on the ground to keep him occupied. I always had a pot of cat treats in my pocket when out in the garden. It was useful to be able to place a few on the ground to keep Hunter busy when I needed to keep him out of the way or to keep Tux and Hunter apart. Despite Hunter biting me I did not hold it against him. I certainly was not going to treat him any differently although I did make sure I was wearing my flowery wellies when he was around. I popped indoors to get Vix some more food and came out to find the pot of cat treats was no longer where I had left it on the garden bench. Vix sat, a vision of complete innocence, in her spot, paws together, squinty smile, waiting patiently. At her feet sat the cat treat pot. Caught on video as I questioned the suspect, it became an iconic moment. Apparently Vix had no idea how they got there. How could anyone not love that fox?

Above: Vix sits innocently beside the cat treat pot

Above: Vix enjoys and egg

On a typically British summer day of wind, rain, and hailstones, Vix stopped by long enough to grab a few pieces of chicken. Her coat did not look as grey as it once had, there were signs of orange in the fur along her back and I was sure her tail was bushier. It was encouraging to see her health improving.

Above: A photo of Vix to show the nose crunckles.

Above: Vix walks through the flowers, again.

Walking through the flowers and over the pots was the route Vix preferred to get to her spot. She showed no appreciation for the results of my gardening endeavours and even plonked herself down on one or two pots resulting in flattened leaves or broken flower stems. Did I mind? Not really. I enjoyed seeing the flowers, but, as with the spring onions, I loved seeing Vix more.

On the second rainy day in a row, I had to content myself with 'playing indoors'. Grey skies did nothing to improve my mood as I continued to sort through Brian's things. I knew I was keeping more of his clothes than was necessary, but every jacket and t-shirt held a memory. Wherever I went on trips to the USA, I brought back a Harley Davidson T shirt for Brian and he had saved them all. Brian had the complete set of books by a favourite author and even as I convinced myself to keep just one, as a book lover I was loathe to split up the set. There were photographs from his childhood and the days before I knew him and piles of paperwork to look through. Arranging the funeral was not the end of the tasks I faced. I had his house to clear and sell and that involved more paperwork and more painful decisions. It seemed all I did was make decisions about throwing things away. It was as if I was slowly getting rid of him. Every memory sparked sadness that he was no longer with me. It was no wonder I spent so much time in the garden. I had bags lined up to go to charity shops when they were able to reopen and eventually took more than sixty bags to shops raising money for Foal Farm Animal Rescue Centre and a local hospice. I knew Brian would appreciate the sale of his possessions being used to raise money to help animals.

Despite being indoors I kept an ever-watchful eye on the garden in case a certain young lady popped by. Suddenly Vix appeared at the window and I realised she knew I was inside the building, presumably in a den of my own. I wondered how she perceived that. The stray cats do the same thing; appear at the window and look inside, waiting. They know 'she' is in there somewhere. I wonder what they think we do inside our homes or how it fits into their view of the world. When Vix looked in, Jem, my youngest cat, was not at all happy to see a 'dog' at the window but Vix seemed completely unphased as Jem's paws scratched at the glass in a failed attempt to get the strange creature to go away. I would not be surprised if I had heard her mumble 'daft cat.' I gave Jem a scritch on the head and went outside to see Vix.

Above: Vix wonders if anyone is home..

Above: Vix is unphased, but Jem is not keen on seeing a 'dog' so close.

Vix returned to the garden later that day, sat in my seat and looked at me through the window once more. How could I resist those big brown eyes? That pleading look? Obviously I could not. I went back into the garden to see her, armed as always, with another treat or two.

The sun, low in the sky, cast the proverbial long shadows of the evening, filling the garden with golden light. It was the photographer's golden hour. Hearing a noise, I looked up and spotted a sparrowhawk being escorted through the neighbourhood by a flock of feral pigeons. The bravery of those birds cannot be underestimated for a plump pigeon is the food of choice for this bird of prey.

Above: Vix gives me an appealing look through the window.

During one of the 'Out to Lunch with Chris and Megs' SIBC broadcasts, Chris Packham said it was best to 'get down to their level' when taking photos of animals so I decided to put the camera on the ground when Vix came by for her second egg and some dog food. It enabled me to get some great close-ups of her tongue, teeth, whiskers, paws, and the ridge on the top of her muzzle (the dorsal meatus) that I referred to as her nose crunkle. It was fascinating to watch how she used her tongue to manoeuvre food and to lap up liquids. When she cleaned her muzzle after eating the tongue almost curls back on itself with amazing dexterity. Chris was right; getting down to their level gives you a whole new perspective on your subject. On warmer days flies appeared in the photos too, zipping across the ground and landing where faint remnants of cat food, chicken or an egg remained.

Above: Vix laps up the dog food.

I do not mind rain, which was just as well because after a long spell of hot, dry weather Britain had entered a rainy period. It is not unexpected, after all we all know how wet it can be during Wimbledon fortnight and that is always in June. It was also a refreshing change. Despite the rain I continued to sit outside as I fed Vix, the water blurring my vision as it bounced off my glasses; someone really has to invent windscreen wipers for spectacle wearers. As often happened when the wind blew Vix was alert to any movement in the undergrowth, the rustling of the leaves or the 'plip' of rain droplets landing on the water butt. Every movement could be a potential predator or prey, a threat, or an opportunity. It must have played havoc with her stress hormones to be constantly on guard. No wonder she appreciated me keeping watch when she slept.

Above: Vix sits in the rain

Above: Vix gives me her most endearing look through the window.

When I next sat down at the laptop, to upload my latest photos and account of Vix's visit, I was in for a shock. There was a message to me on the SIBC Facebook page from Chris Packham. *The* Chris Packham. The man himself! I had been summoned...from above. Well, maybe not from above but it was a huge honour to be mentioned by Chris.

The message read:

Marion Veal – Cate has messaged you on Facebook – please check your messages. Thank you!

Cate turned out to be Cate Crocker, Chris' Personal Assistant, and a lovely lady. It may have been Cate who sent the message but she never revealed that to me so I shall live with the honour of being contacted by the SIBC founder himself. Before long Cate and I were chatting on the telephone like old friends, talking about the SIBC, how it was nice to see such positive stories and beautiful photographs during an awful time and of course we mentioned Vix. Chris and Megs were going to do another live broadcast and they wanted to feature Vix. Hmm, I was not sure she would be willing to be interviewed live but... Apparently, they would not need to interview Vix, they would just be showing one of my videos and Lucy Chapmen would talk about my foxy friend and all she meant to the SIBC. It was so exciting but...a secret until the broadcast was announced. Mum's the word. Once again, this beautiful fox was bringing me new experiences. She really had changed my life in so many ways.

When Vix arrived for the second time the next day it was clear that she was tired. She sat down in her favourite spot but there were noises in neighbouring gardens, children played on a trampoline, the breeze blew the foliage in the flowerpots and she could not settle. Her head dropped, her eyes closed and then sprang open again at the slightest sound. I watched as her eyelids grew heavy and then, opened yet again. I had my book with me so I spoke to her in my gentlest voice, informing Vix I would sit with her and read, and she could have a snooze knowing that I would keep watch. She did not have to fight the need for sleep anymore, I was there. Perhaps it was the tone of my voice that conveyed the message but whatever it was she seemed reassured by my presence and soon her eyes closed once more, and she dozed off.

Above: Vix takes the opportunity to rest, knowing she is safe in my garden

It continued to be a huge honour to see Vix fall asleep when I was there. I knew she was rushed off her paws trying to provide for her cubs and if I could give her a moment of safety to recharge those foxy batteries I would. I had now read several books about wildlife and foxes. Amazon was delivering a new one almost every couple of days. As I sat and read with Vix beside me, I found myself relaxing too. The tension left my shoulders and the tightness in my jaw, that was a constant companion since Brian died, eased. My own sleep had been erratic for the past couple of years, a result of the menopause and the constant worry about Brian. Vix and I were helping each other, in fact had I not been on sentry duty, I would have happily curled up beside her and dozed too. Every now and then Vix would open an eye and look in my direction but, seeing me still there, she adjusted her position, curled her tail a little tighter around her body and closed her eyes. I reassured her that she was safe. It seemed to be enough.

On 10th June 2020 Boris Johnson revealed five tests the UK had to pass to avoid a second spike in Covid-19 infections. Having evaluated the risks the government decided that non-essential shops could finally reopen on 15th June 2020. Groups of up to six people could meet in open spaces and single households could form a support bubble with another household. Anyone who had been shielding would still need to continue to do so but, there was a sense of relief that some form of normality was about to return. Things were looking up.

Above: Vix enjoys an egg and dog food.

Above: Vix checks it is safe to approach.

Above: Vix, the Lockdown Fox

I do not know how a fox tells the time, but Vix regularly turned up around 4.30pm. I would hear the familiar clatter of paws on the fence and there she was dropping down into the garden. When Vix had not appeared by 5.30pm I grew concerned. If something happened to her would I ever find out? Unless a body turned up in the road and I happened to see it, Vix would just stop visiting and I would never know why. I contemplated talking to the road sweeper and asking him to keep an eye out for any dead or injured foxes and letting me know if he found any. Vix was not just any fox, she was my friend. If she had been microchipped, I could have tracked her using GPS or similar. Unfortunately, her life beyond my garden would remain a mystery. If something happened to her, I wanted to know.

Vix finally arrived at 5.50pm and although I told her how worried I had been she appeared unconcerned. She received the offered chicken gratefully and took pieces away. When she returned, I was indoors, and she peered at me through the window with what can only be described as puppy dog eyes. I went out to feed her once more and when my back was turned, she moved swiftly and was last seen legging it over the fence with the pot of cat treats held tight between her teeth. I could almost hear her laughing in triumph. She finally had them! Cheeky fox!

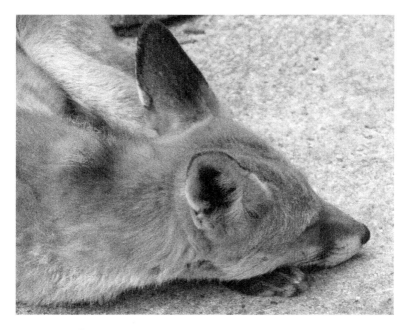

Above: Time for a rest

The next day, Vix played it innocent about the cat treats despite having been spotted leaving the scene of the crime with them in her mouth. No DNA fingerprinting or identity parade was needed, but she called into question the impartiality of the only witness. Apparently, I must have been mistaken and she certainly was not about to admit to being unable to open the pot with her teeth and paws once back at her hide-out. She poked her tongue out at me although some people tell me that is a sign of affection in dogs. As if to prove she had a clear conscience she promptly fell asleep as I sat with her. It gave me a chance to admire her now re-growing beautiful fur. Is it orange or a rusty red? Whichever you choose the colour of red fox fur is uniquely beautiful.

English and French lavender turned the borders purple and Osteospermums filled the garden with cheerful daisy flowers. Sparrows perched on the roses searching for the aphids farmed by the colony of ants living under the decking and the solar-powered oxygenator created a frantic plume of bubbles in the pond. My husband's statue of Saint Francis of Assisi, continued to cast a caring eye on the animals in the garden. It made me ponder again on the forces that had sent Vix to me.

Usually, Vix and I encountered each other in the back garden so it was a surprise one day to find her strolling by as I was tidying up at the front of the house. I could moan like Victor Meldrew, from the television series One Foot in the Grave, about the items that turn up in my front garden. I have no idea where the continued supply of dryer sheets comes from, but someone clearly uses far more than they can keep track of. I also find cigarette butts, crisp packets, drink cans, sweet wrappers and more. The fast-food industry has a lot to answer for when it comes to litter. As I muttered about the selfish nature of some people there was Vix walking nonchalantly along the pavement. She gave me a confused look, perhaps because this was not where she expected to find me. I was the lady who lived in the garden at the back of the houses, so this could not possibly be the same woman.

I said, 'Hello, Vix. What are you doing here?"

She was probably thinking the same thing. Vix gave me a long look, then, clearly far too busy to stop and chat, left her mark at the base of a nearby tree before heading off along the pavement in that jaunty fox style and I watched her fluffy tail disappear into a hedge.

Above: My garden was always a safe place to relax.

Above: Vix in her spot.

The day of the new SIBC broadcast and Vix's star performance was fast approaching. I thought it best to warn Vix that one of my videos had been shown as part of the promotional video broadcast on Facebook. I wanted her to prepare for the fame that would surely follow the internet exposure. She was unimpressed. For my part, now that the upcoming broadcast had been mentioned on the SIBC Facebook page, and Vix had appeared in the trailer, I felt able to talk about it should anyone ask.

Above: Are you awake?

When Vix wandered off I took the opportunity to sit in a garden chair, in the sunshine, and do what people of a certain age are entitled to do. I closed my eyes and had a doze. With so much still to do for Brian I often felt guilty about doing 'nothing' but I was tired and I needed to close my eyes. I was still conscious of the sounds around me as I drifted in and out of that twilight world of almost sleep. Bees buzzed, sparrows twittered, children bounced on trampolines. You would never know that a deadly virus was striking fear throughout the world as I dozed in my garden that afternoon. For a while I let myself relax and the sounds of nature soothed me. And then I felt a cool, wet something gently touching my knee. I woke to see Vix sniffing me. She was so gentle and inquisitive. What was I doing, her gaze asked? Why were my eyes closed? Why was I not sitting where I usually sat?

"Hello, Vix," I said softly, my voice fresh from sleep.

She hopped up onto the metal bench and looked down at me with those lovely smiley eyes. I could almost hear her ask, "What are you doing?"

So of course, I explained. "I was having a doze in the afternoon sunshine. You often have one, so I thought I would too."

"Got anything to eat?"

She knew I did and having hoisted myself out of the chair I went in search of something tasty for her. As Vix nibbled on the latest offering, I admired her tail, now considerably fuller and fluffier than it had been a few weeks ago. There were a few grass seeds trapped in the fur, but it was no longer that sad thin stick from before.

Above: Vix's tail fuller and fluffier.

Above: Vix laps up her egg.

Above: Vix and Mew wait patiently for me to finish teaching.

I wondered what would be said about Vix in the SIBC broadcast. I shared my thoughts with her, after all she had a vested interest in the programme, but the fox was more concerned with what was available to eat. I suppose superstars like Vix get used to all the attention and it was like water off a fox's back. When she returned later, Vix peered in the window and as I was teaching at the time, I could only give her a wave, which just seemed to confuse her. Perhaps Mew was able to communicate to her, through the window, that she would have to wait for food, because they both settled down for the duration of the Skype call. The small piece of decking Vix snoozed on was made for me by Brian from an old pallet and a couple of decking tiles. The stray cats also seem to like sleeping on it, perhaps because it is off the ground, or because those extra centimetres of height allow them to look in the window at Mew and Jem. Whatever the reason, it is nice to provide all my visitors with somewhere they feel safe and whenever I look at it, I think of Brian, he is everywhere in the things he made or the little jobs he did for me around the home.

Despite the pleasure being part of the SIBC gave me on some days I did not want to get out of bed. Partly it was due to the bed clothes making themselves extra snuggly but mostly it was because I did not want to face the day. There were days when I was sapped of strength both physically and emotionally. Getting out of a chair took effort. I forced myself to brush my hair, to get dressed and put on a smile despite a voice in my head asking 'what was the point?'. I had Mew and Jem to think of and I would never abandon them but my world had changed. A dark cloud hung over everything. I had lost direction, my focus, and there was nothing on the horizon to look forward to. Even booked trips to the theatre in the summer had already been cancelled or postponed for a year. I did not want to be reminded that Brian was gone; to have to look at more paperwork; to call another company and tell them he was dead. I did not want to sort through another bag or box of Brian's possessions and decide what to keep and what to throw away; to look at yet more things that reminded me of the man and the life I had lost. I wanted to go somewhere with Brian; to sit beside him as he drove along the country lanes of Kent he had cycled as a boy; to see some animals or walk together on a beach, then stop somewhere for a cup of tea and a toasted tea cake on the way home. That was never going to happen again. That life was over. Mew and Jem walking backwards and forwards over my duvet-covered body reminded me that I still had responsibilities. I had to get up, face the day and, more importantly, feed the cats. I threw back the bed clothes. It was a matter of putting one foot in front of the other, living in the moment and dealing with one task at a time. It was time to get up and put the kettle on.

Friday 19th June 2020

The SIBC Live broadcast took place. I was mentioned and Vix was shown in the video sitting beside the treat pot she had 'acquired' as Lucy Chapman explained Vix's story and how I was helping her heal. Friends messaged me, excited they had seen the broadcast and it was a moment of happiness in a year marred by sadness. Vix was not so impressed. There would be no truckload of chicken and eggs arriving any time soon. On arriving in the garden on broadcast day, she wandered through the flowers before settling down in her favourite spot to sleep. I pottered about quietly so as not to wake her. Even superstars need their rest.

Above: A smiley face through the flowers.

Above: Vix rests her chin on the bark chippings.

23rd June 2020

We had become used to the daily announcements on the BBC of the number of Covid infections in the UK, the number of people in intensive care, the daily number of deaths and the total death toll. It was surreal. Those of us who were fans of the television series The Walking Dead had been preparing ourselves for the zombie apocalypse but this was beginning to feel more like being part of 'Survivors' a 1970's British television series about the spread of a deadly disease. Prime minister Boris Johnson, in a Downing Street briefing, revealed further changes to the national lockdown. From 4th July 2020 pubs, restaurants and hairdressers would reopen provided they adhered to the government guidelines on social distancing. The self-cut hairstyles, seen all over Skype and Zoom, were soon to become a thing of the past. Things were looking up. Maybe I would get a trip out after all.

I had noticed that with so many people now out and about at the weekend, particularly on Saturday, Vix came by less often. I assumed that she was not keen on so much activity and there was certainly more traffic on the roads. I feared for her safety but there was nothing I could do, she was a wild animal and it was her right to go where she wanted, even if that meant crossing a busy road.

Above: Vix ponders how to pick up an egg

There was a grass seed stuck in the fur on the right side of Vix's face, the next time I saw her. I hoped she would be able to remove it with a well-placed paw. If she trusted me enough to let me brush her it would have been gone in no time. I would love to have stroked her, to find out what that gorgeous orange fur felt like. Vix's needs always came before my own and making her accustomed to a human touching her was not likely to help her in the long run, so I never tried. Once again when Vix settled down, in her preferred corner of the garden, I did my best to reassure her, she was in a safe place for a snooze, with or without an annoying grass seed.

Above: Vix shows off her improving physique.

Above: A grass seed in her fur.

Above: Vix looking a little forlorn.

I had always wanted a garden pond having studied invertebrate zoology as part of my university degree course. I can still spot *Asellus*, the water louse and *Gammarus pulex*, the freshwater shrimp. I have a soft spot for Planarian flatworms and love a ramshorn snail. I finally built a pond the summer after my Mum died; the summer I had the builders in, and Mew turned up. I had chosen a spot on the lawn to dig and in went the shovel. If I were to build it again, I would dig a deeper hole, but it seemed deep enough at the time when I was huffing and puffing, and turning a bright shade of beetroot, as I shovelled soil and piled it high at the side of the pond. I stood a stick up in the centre, imagining it full of water and thought "This'll do". When I stood on the liner in my socked feet it still seemed a reasonable depth but in hindsight, I should have kept going. I should have had a glass of water, allowed my skin to return to a normal shade and dug a little deeper. It could do with being another foot deep. I keep the water topped up, with as much rainwater as buckets around the garden can collect, although during the summer the rate of evaporation proves a challenge. Water boatman, water louse, leaches, and a large herd of ramshorn snails roam around the liner and through the tangle of plant stems and roots. However, it does not seem to attract amphibians. A frog turned up the second year the pond existed but did not stay; at least I never saw it again. Tadpoles, given to me by a friend, disappeared although I did find a few baby toads in the garden later in the year. The local cats drink at it and so do the foxes. I could happily spend the afternoon pond dipping. The ramshorn snails sweep like a herd of wildebeest across the algae. A turned stone reveals leeches, lashing around for something new to latch on to, and a flash of silver signalled the presence of a water boatman with a bubble of oxygen trapped close to its body. Water louse and shrimps scuttled beneath the stones, under floating leaves and through the curly growth of *Elodea*, the Canadian pond weed. My pond remained devoid of amphibians, but it was still full of other aquatic life.

Many SIBC members wanted to know if I put out water for Vix. I explained that I had a water dish for cats and birds as well as the pond and Vix obliged with a pond-side photoshoot, her tongue making ripples in the water as she quenched her thirst.

Above: Vix takes a drink at the pond..

Giving Vix large bits of chicken was not the most helpful thing I could do but it would be a while before I had the blatantly obvious idea to cut it up. I assumed a fox would want a lot of food, would be eating large pieces every day and chomping it to pieces would be simple. In fact, Vix preferred small pieces of chompy-chicken and enjoyed it with bone-crunching relish. In hindsight knowing her usual diet consisted of small rodents and birds, the pieces I gave her were much too large.

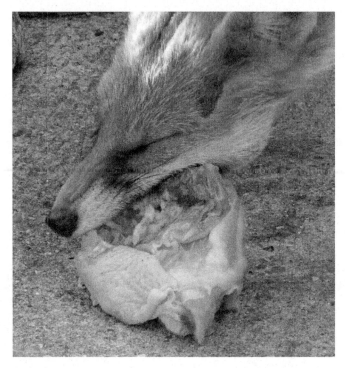

Above: The chicken – before I thought to cut it smaller.

"Cor! What a scorcher!"

June 2020 had some very hot days, and it was clear Vix was feeling the effect of the heat. When a dog pants the evaporation of moisture from the surface of its tongue helps to cool it down. Vix would do the same, her long tongue lolling to one side as she gaped open mouthed. Dogs also sweat through their paws, but I had not seen any tell-tale damp pad marks on the concrete to confirm that it was the same for foxes. Vix was still a busy mum and the combination of her parenting responsibilities, and the heat of the day were exhausting. When Vix decided it was time to flake out somewhere safe, she did just that.

Above: A very hot fox.

Above: Vix worn out by the heat of the day..

A friend had sent me a link to a pet pool with the message that I might like to buy one for Vix. It was meant as a joke, but it planted a seed of an idea in my mind. I Googled the make and liked what I discovered. You did not have to inflate the pool; it had rigid sides and unfolded concertina style. I thought back to all those summer days, long ago, when my parents used a foot pump to inflate our childhood paddling pool and I wondered why no one had invented this foldable pool sooner. It would have saved a lot of effort and on occasions when the foot pump was not to hand, a lot of human puff. Sometimes it takes a while to hit on the obvious.

The decision was easily made. If Vix was feeling particularly hot she might like to paddle in a pool of cooling water or even sit down in it. I sent for the pool. When it arrived, I set it up in the garden near the pond. It was on a route I knew she travelled around my garden, so she was sure to encounter it. I half-filled it with water and carried on pottering about in the garden waiting for Vix to arrive. In the vegetable plot, the spring onions were doing well despite being sat on by a fox. The leeks had grown tall and the tomatoes had ripened. I picked small cherry tomatoes off the plants and ate them, savouring that moment they burst in my mouth. There was nothing quite like the flavour of something picked fresh from the plant.

It is very satisfying to grow your own fruit and vegetables. Over the years I have tried different varieties with equal measure of success and failure. I know I cannot grow carrots, beetroot and sweet potatoes but I can grow ordinary potatoes in abundance. Each year I try something new and this year it was the turn of mangetout. I had created a web of canes and string to support them and the neighbouring pea plants and they had woven their tendrils tightly around them. It was always a pleasure to pick a pod from the plant and crack it open to reveal the swollen peas inside, and then pop them straight into my mouth. You could not get anything fresher than that. I hoped the mange tout would prove equally successful. The strawberries, despite being covered in flowers eventually produced a poor show of fruit; some years you get a good crop and some years you do not, a gardener gets used to the vagaries of nature and the effect of the previous winter. In a similar vein it did not look as if there were going to be many apples on the tree this year. The tree, my mother planted, has three different varieties grafted onto one root stock. In a good year I am able to eat Desiree apples straight from the tree and make apple crumble with James Grieve and Bramley apples. I also had the small apple tree I brought back from Brian's garden and I was excited to see three apples developing. The pear tree, on which the bird feeders hung, was covered in fruit too. It was going to be a good pear year if not an apple one. There was always something to look forward to in a garden.

When Vix turned up I kept a casual eye on her. She approached the strange new object I had placed on top of the bark chippings and gave it a sniff. It was pronounced 'harmless' and she leaned over the edge. By now I had my camera in my hand willing her to step into the water and frolic. I definitely hoped for a bit of foxy frolicking. I focussed on her, sending a telepathic message, "Step into the water, step into the water."

Above: Vix drinks from the pet pool.

Vix was clearly neither telepathic nor the frolicking kind. She had a few long drinks of water and then padded down the garden towards me. The pool had served its purpose in providing refreshment. It was also to have an added benefit for me. Several times during the hot weather that followed I placed the pool in the garden, filled it up and stepped in and out of it throughout the day for a paddle and a cool down. It was very refreshing on the feet and if I could not get to the beach at least I could pretend I was there when I paddled in the fox pool. For anyone reading in the Americas paddling in the UK is what you call wading. I do not want you to think I set out across the pool in a canoe. It was not that big. Although I love a Canadian canoe and was taught to paddle one properly in Ontario, Canada. Brian always called them 'unstable craft' but I love them and one of my happiest memories is paddling one, single-handed, on Moraine Lake in Alberta. Floating on the water surrounded by the mountains was something to treasure.

Above: Shhh, let a sleeping fox lie.

Belonging to the SIBC Facebook page had also renewed my interest in nature writing and I sent away for several books about wildlife: many, coincidently, with the word 'fox' in their title. I was learning a lot about foxes from studying the lady herself but also from my reading. I informed Vix of some of the interesting facts I had discovered as she sat beside me. She gave me a look, appearing to inform me, in the politest possible terms, that I was not telling her anything she did not already know.

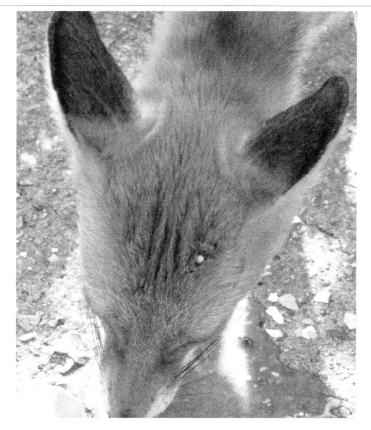

Above: Vix sporting a tick in her fur.

When Vix bent down to lap up an egg I spotted a couple of small white flecks in the fur on her head, they were clearly not grass seeds, and I wondered if they might be ticks. Sure-enough over the coming days they increased in size confirming their identity.

Ticks are parasitic, egg-shaped arachnids. They tend to attach to a animal around the head, ears, and feet, no doubt where there is a good blood supply close to the surface of the skin. Once hooked on they pierce the flesh with their mouth parts, some of which have barbs on them to prevent easy extraction. The parasites become larger, and thus more visible, as they fill with blood. Ticks carry infections and one of the reasons a special tick removal tool should be used is to prevent blood from their gut, and the bacteria within it, entering the host's blood as they are pulled off. Lyme disease, a bacterial infection, which can affect dogs and humans is carried by ticks and, if you frequent grassland or areas grazed by sheep and deer, you are advised to keep a look out for ticks on your clothing or body. For the ticks to have become visible on Vix's head they must have been there for some time enjoying their blood meal. Once sated the ticks fall off on their own. I wondered what, if anything, I could do about them but when Vix returned, they had disappeared, so it seemed I did not have to worry after all. However, there soon appeared another obvious one on the top of her head above her left eye. I returned to my research.

As I had never touched Vix, and was not about to wrestle with her, removing ticks using a specially designed tool was not going to be an option. I needed something I could add to her food. The tick would most likely fall off on its own, just as the others had, but if it was knocked off or scratched by Vix it could lead to an infection which I did not want her to have to suffer. I telephoned the Fox Project and spoke to a lady who suggested I try giving Vix a very small quantity of crushed garlic in a honey and jam sandwich. Fortunately, I had some garlic and honey. I crushed the garlic clove, mixed it with honey and smoothed it onto a piece of bread. I offered it to Vix, she sniffed it and promptly rejected it. I did inform her that foxes were renowned for having a sweet tooth and that the garlic inside would help remove the tick but apparently it was not to her liking. At least I tried.

Above: What's that on the end of her nose?

Above: Downward dog. Vix practicing yoga in my garden.

Above: Who broke the egg?

Over the next couple of days, the tick enlarged as it gorged on Vix's blood but then, once its appetite had been sated, it disappeared.

I continued to drive back and forth to Brian's house, clocking up the miles on my car as I did so. On the journey towards his house the memories would flood back and overwhelm me. I was soon sobbing my heart out as I drove. I had to prepare myself for that flood of emotions every time. When I finally opened the shed in Brian's garden to remove his bike it proved another emotional moment. The bike was the essence of Brian. He had cycled since he was a small child; had cycled all over Kent and as a young boy made it all the way to London's Tower Bridge, which gives you an idea of how little traffic there was on the roads in those days. I stood the bike up, fumbling with the kickstand as I did so. Brian would have rolled his eyes at me. I rested a hand on the saddle, then placed it around the handlebars and imagined Brian's hand there too. I remembered when he bought the bike and the thrill it gave me to see him ride it. I have given his two fold-up bikes, tools and accessories to a local bike project for adults with special needs but I still have Brian's bike. It meant so much to him. He was a born cyclist.

I was not a cyclist. When given the opportunity to switch from my tricycle, with a metal box on the back, to the two-wheeler my brother had grown out of, I chose my tricycle. It was due to that childhood decision that I grew up not able to ride a bike. I finally decided to learn in adulthood. I bought a bike with a basket on the front and named her Daisy. We took Daisy to the local park and with Brian running along behind me I peddled like crazy until he was able to let go and I was off on my own. As I cycled one way around the park, I passed a little girl, probably no more than seven years old, riding the other way. She had stabilisers on her bike. We gave each other encouragement each time we passed.

However, life as a cyclist was not for me. To start with nobody warned me how painful it would be on the nether regions and Daisy had a propensity of veering to the right causing me to crash into a telegraph pole. It later transpired that there was a fault in her frame but by then her basket was bent, and I had hung up my cycle helmet. Although cycling was not for me it was Brian's passion and watching the Tour de France became a must. The Tour de France normally took place in June and July and Brian watched it religiously every year. Even when we were in Canada, he was able to find a channel broadcasting it live. I would wake to the sound of commentator Phil Liggett informing us how far behind the lead riders the peloton was, who was wearing the yellow jersey and which rider had been named King of the mountains.

Le Tour de France 2020 was scheduled to take place from the 27th June to the 19th July, but due to Covid it was postponed until 29th August to 20th September. It was strange not to hear the familiar music nor see the mass of cyclists zooming through the French countryside.

I loaded Brian's bike into the car, with the help of one of his neighbours, and drove home.

I loved the fact that Vix would look for me through the window. It would be interesting to know what went through her mind as she did so, but I doubt it was anything more than a desire for food and finding the lady who provided it. It would be nice to think she was grateful that I fed her and offered a safe place to rest; that she felt something akin to pleasure in my company but that would be anthropomorphising. However, her closed eyes, her licking tongue, that squinty smile and relaxed demeanour suggested she was happy to share the garden with me.

Above: Vix waits on the garden bench.

Above: Vix checks to see who is at home.

The hot days turned into windy ones with the wind gusting through the garden shaking plants violently and blowing over flowerpots. The windchimes clattered frantically in the branches of the magnolia tree. This did not seem to prevent Vix from settling down in a favourite spot, stretching out her front legs and having an afternoon nap, although the constant twitching of her ears suggested she was aware of movements around her. Sometimes she would rest her chin on her outstretched legs and other times nestle it into the bark chippings on the ground. I assumed the chippings absorbed the sun's heat and provided a warm bed to lie on.

Above: Legs stretched out enjoying the sunshine.

Above: Vix knew where she was safe.

We were still isolating from Covid-19 on the last day of June 2020 and a work-related issue had upset me. With no one around to talk to, my cats were told all about it but, as they were unable to give me their unbiased opinion on the matter it was left circling around in my mind raising my anxiety levels. With fewer distractions small issues became big ones for many of us, blowing out of all proportion. More people, also isolated, were reaching out to others, often strangers, for help and to hear another human voice. The SIBC proved a haven for many of its members on anxious days. The sight of a friendly garden bird, a blurred photo taken in excitement of a kingfisher or a stunning barn owl sweeping across a meadow brought a smile, a laugh or a gasp of awe. The natural world may have created a deadly virus, but it was also providing us with a solution to our anxieties and a way to feel at peace.

To clear my mind, I decided to water the plants that grow in a plot alongside the drive at the front of my house. It was nice to get a breath of air, albeit one polluted with traffic fumes. I looked up and down the road, waved to a distant neighbour and then to my surprise I saw a fox running through the garden of a house opposite mine. I stood still and watched. It was not Vix. I caught another glimpse of the fox. It was much smaller than Vix and had a very bushy tail. I dashed indoors, grabbed my camera and was back out in the street in less than a minute. Where was the fox?

Nothing moved. Had I lost it? I scoured the gardens and waited. Cars drove by at speed. A large red double decker bus blocked my view but when I could see the gardens opposite again there it was, just a flash of rust coloured fur but it was still there. I stared at the foliage of a privet hedge as I walked along the road and the fox popped its head through a hole in the branches and stepped onto the pavement. I beamed with excitement. The fox was a youngster. Its fur was pale orange, the black markings on its front legs distinct and the two black areas of fur on either side of its muzzle were larger and darker than in adults. It was beautiful and so fluffy. And, oh that tail tipped with white! Could this be one of Vix's cubs? I so wanted it to be one of hers.

I received curious looks from a couple of passers-by as I stood on the pavement, camera in hand staring at the other side of the street. What on earth was this woman doing? Was I a snooper?

Had I misunderstood the meaning of neighbourhood watch? Or perhaps I was a private investigator intent on catching one of the residents up to something? I doubt anyone thought any of these things, but I certainly looked a tad odd. I did not care about the looks I received; I was a woman on a mission. I aimed my zoom lens across the road. I was not focused on the houses but on a beautiful wild fox cub. The little fox walked along the pavement parallel to the hedge and I kept pace from my side of the road. It stopped and looked at the road.

"Please don't try to cross! Please don't try to cross! Please don't try to cross!" I muttered like an urgent mantra.

I was already preparing myself to walk out and stop the traffic if the fox attempted to do so, but the cub decided against it and disappeared through another hedge, dashed across a front garden and down the alley that ran between two houses. It was gone but I was thrilled, there is no other word for it. This was probably one of Vix's cubs and it was a beauty. As ever, nature had taken my mind completely off the bad news of the day and filled me with excitement.

When Vix came by later I mentioned I had seen a cub and asked if it was hers. In typical diva fashion she gave nothing away as she feasted on an egg.

A Fluffy young fox cub is spotted.

JULY 2020

The Fox year- July

As the cubs become more independent, they will need to find food for themselves. As part of their continuing education into the way of being a fox, the adults share the responsibility of taking their young to known feeding sites.

July started with rain. It may have officially been summer, but the weather had clearly not received the memo, so rain it did and heavily. Vix still turned up, rain or not. I put on my waterproof jacket and sat outside with her. The things you do for the ones you love. The rain ran off my waterproof's hood, blurred the vision through my glasses, soaked my trousers but glistened on Vix's coat and it did not seem to bother her at all. She tucked into her egg, lapping happily at both the yoke and the egg white. In typical British weather fashion, the next day the sun came out. The memo had finally arrived.

Above: Vix, never sure whether to have the yoke or egg white first..

Above: A mid-day yawn.

Above: Vix peeps from behind the bird fountain.

Despite lockdown, and it being the school summer holidays, I was still teaching by Skype and was online to a student when Vix appeared. Her unpredictability always made her arrival a pleasant surprise. Sometimes I would look up from the computer and she would be sitting waiting for me and giving me a squinty smile. The students I taught were used to me telling them about the fox that visited my garden and asking to be excused for a few moments so that I could go out and give Vix something to eat. Pausing whilst she fed the fox was just another part of lessons with Marion.

As I explained to Vix what was on the menu today, I held out the box containing an egg and a small piece of chicken. I asked Vix which she wanted. She sniffed the offerings, and her nose brushed my fingers and she licked them. Her small warm tongue connecting with my skin was a surprise and a thrill. A nose bump from Vix was always welcome but a lick was something special. The mere act of her touching me warmed my heart. If it was a 'thank you' she was more than welcome.

Above: Vix investigates my fingers.

Above: Vix demonstrates the flexibility of her tongue..

Foxes are a conundrum in the animal world. They are canines, related to domestic dogs but have feline characteristics too. The pupils in their eyes are vertical slits like a cat and they are equally agile. Much has been written about the ability of foxes to adapt to new environments, particularly as humans continue to encroach on their natural habitat. It is to their credit that they are able to negotiate our gardens, with their ponds, gnomes and various fences. With a lick of my hand, Vix, had shown that wild or domesticated, the connection between species was the same.

Above: High on the garden fence.

Lockdown in the United Kingdom eased on 4th July 2020. Pubs, restaurants, and cafés were open for business once more. You could go out and eat a meal you had not cooked yourself, provided you still adhered to social distancing rules. Museums, cinemas, and theme parks were open too. You could stay in a hotel, go camping and, joy of joys, you could get your hair cut. Those of us with our natural hair colour showing through in our roots were grateful for the chance to get them dyed once more. It felt as if normality, however slowly, was returning for us all.

On the 5th July 2020 I looked out into the garden and saw two foxes. I looked again searching for the tell-tale markings that would identify my friend, the scar on her left temple and that squinty smile. Vix was definitely one of the foxes and the other was…. oh, my goodness, it was the young fox I had seen across the road at the end of June, less than a week ago. Vix had brought her cub to my garden!

I was beside myself with emotion and excitement.

Vix sat, patiently, looking towards the back door waiting for me to appear. I tried to stay calm, grabbed the food bag I always had ready along with my camera and headed for the door. I opened it gently, speaking quietly to Vix as I stepped outside. I did not want to frighten the young fox away. Without looking directly at the cub, I sat down on the garden bench, flowery wellies neatly together. Vix approached me but the cub hid nervously behind the vegetable patch, ears sticking up above the foliage. Hunter one of the stray cats was nearby and Vix chased him off. It was the first time she had approached the cat; the first time she had shooed him away. She was every inch the mother defending her cub and not to be messed with by a cat. Sensibly, Hunter slunk away and Vix came closer to me. Her eyes closed in a slow blink and she gave me her characteristic squinty smile. As had become our routine, I returned the gesture. Gradually the cub padded closer. Vix walked over to him and encouraged him closer still as if telling him it was all right; this human could be trusted. Feeling braver now that his Mum was nearby the cub approached me. They stood side by side, Vix smiling proudly, as if to say "Look, this is my son." I spoke softly to them both and then Vix walked off, leaving her cub with me as she disappeared over the fence.

She had left her cub with me. Breathe, Marion, breathe. She trusted me enough to leave her cub with me! Stay calm, Marion, stay calm. Apparently I was to be his human 'aunty'.

The cub approached me, and I tried to contain my excitement and not scare it off.

"Hello, you're Fluffy, aren't you," I said, and he was, his fur and tail were just that.

Fluffy, as the cub came to be called, sniffed the blue flowerpots, looked at me, dashed away, then came back again, checking to see if what his Mum had said about me was true, that I was to be trusted. When Vix came back the cub clambered over the flowerpots just like his mother did. Clearly foxes are not born gardeners. I put down some dog food and chicken pieces. Fluffy made eye contact with me and then ate some chicken. Bravely, he came even closer. I talked soothingly to the little fox as he ate. Tears welled up in my eyes. Vix trusted me with her baby. There was no greater honour or privilege.

Above: I would like you to meet my son.

Above: Vix introduces me to Fluffy.

Above: Vix shows her son around the garden.

Mother and cub posed for a family photograph or two before disappearing over the fence leaving me lost for words. What can you say when a wild animal brings her cub to your garden in broad daylight? When a wild animal, who trusts you enough to sleep in your presence, brings her baby to see you and reassures it that it is all right to approach this human? That this human will look after you and give you food. That you are safe with this human when I leave you alone with her. Vix had shown me just how much she trusted me, and it was beyond special. I was humbled and ecstatic. Vix knew me but Fluffy did not; he was truly wild, and yet under his mother's instruction he approached me. That was incredibly special. I am not ashamed to say that later that day I cried and this time they were tears of joy.

The next day I was still buzzing with the excitement of Vix bringing her baby to see me. I still did not know if the cub was a boy or a girl although my instinct told me it was a boy. Vix arrived in the afternoon, alone and, having taken yesterday's visit in her stride, stayed to have some chompy-chicken. She took some away and I assumed that was for Fluffy. Was he her only cub? The dog fox may have taken others off exploring but throughout her time with me I felt certain Vix was raising her family alone; that there was no dog fox supporting her, she was a single mum. If that was the case, then Fluffy was her only offspring. I kept looking out of the window in case Vix came back and her cub appeared again. And then there she was and Fluffy was with her. He met my gaze, his eyes bright and inquisitive. I was an immensely proud human aunty. Fluffy looked healthy and it was good to know that at least one of Vix's cubs had survived despite her brush with mange. Of course, now I had two foxes to worry about and extra food to buy. What a wonderful 'burden'.

Above: Fluffy

Above: Vix showing little regard for my planting.

Above: Vix in the golden afternoon light.

Sadly, Fluffy did not accompany Vix into my garden again when I was there. It was as if she had brought Fluffy to show him where he could find a ready supply of food if he needed it. The lesson had been taught and there were others to move on to. I was like a mother hen wondering where he was. Was our little boy all right? Vix came by early in the evening and would still take chicken away but where was Fluffy? Did Vix tell him to stay home because it was raining? Was Fluffy already off on his own searching for food or was Vix still taking food back? There were so many unanswered questions. I decided it was time to set up the night camera again.

The next time Vix visited she wanted to sit closer to me which was a surprise and even my camera received a friendly a nose bump in her eagerness to be near me. She sat, not in her usual place, but on my tiny piece of decking, closer than normal. I would like to think it was her way of saying "Thank you for looking after my son. I am relieved to know you will keep him safe." That's me anthropomorphising again. I would like to think I had passed another test. Whatever the reason, it was not something I took lightly, nor intended to exploit.

As always, where Vix sat and how close she came to me was her choice and never something I manipulated.

Above: Vix gets even closer to the house.

I started to think about the months ahead and what might happen to Vix and Fluffy when winter arrived. With that in mind I sent away for a larger version of the cat shelters. I already had three shelters for use by any passing stray cat, in various places around the garden. Tux seemed to like them the most and had spent time in each one testing it out for comfort. When the much larger version arrived, I assembled it with moderate ease and the use of only a couple of choice swear words. I positioned it in the garden and put some chicken inside hoping to encourage Vix to investigate the weird new object. When Vix arrived, she spotted the new 'kennel' and gave it a good sniff. Vix found the chicken inside and took it away. At least she knew the shelter existed should she need it. I placed the shelter at the bottom of the garden under the apple tree next to the shedlette. I could see the entrance from the house and would be able to spot if anyone took up residence.

The next day I looked out and found Vix standing on the shelter with her nose in the apple tree. I think it gave her a better view of the bird feeder, much to the annoyance of my feathered friends. Having given the apple tree and bird feeders a good foxy sniff Vix's fur was covered in woolly aphid. At least the shelter was proving useful for her to access new areas if not to shelter in.

Above: To let, one fox shelter.

Above: Red fox and sunflowers..

Above: A chewy piece of chicken.

Vix began to reduce her time with me; not staying in the garden for as long as she used to nor visiting as often. Her job as a mother was coming to an end and Fluffy was learning to make his own way in the world of foxes. I knew one of my neighbours also left food out for Vix so with fewer mouths to feed she obviously did not need to scavenge so often. It comforted me to know others were looking after her, but I was saddened by the thought that our time together was growing shorter and may even come to an end. Vix was such a huge personality and an enormous part of my life and my friend. I looked forward to her daily visits and the comfort we gave each other.

Above: Vix claims my place on the bench.

Above: Is that another tick?

Above: Vix assumes a familiar pose.

It was strange that Vix had begun to sit closer to me since her visit with Fluffy. Sometimes I could have reached out my hand and touched her. The desire to feel that foxy fur beneath my fingers was strong. I wanted to make that final connection between us. I love stroking Mew and Jem and sharing nose bumps. We may not be able to communicate by speech, but we can convey our love for each other through contact. Holding Brian's hand had brought us both unspoken comfort. Heads placed forehead to forehead conveys a wealth of understanding and emotions. I wanted to give Vix a message in fox language. I longed to touch Vix's back and give her a gentle stroke, but I never did. Vix was not a pet, and I did not want to be the one to cross that invisible line. So far, all contact between us had been instigated by Vix and that was how it had to be. For me, the reward was being able to spend time with her and watching her grow ever healthier. To watch her fur turn from grey to orange; to see her tail grow fluffier. However, just when I thought I had experienced all the warm and fuzzy moments I was going to have, Vix would do something new that made me feel soft inside. In mid-July after having some chompy-chicken she settled down close to me on my tiny piece of decking, stretched out her elegant legs and fell asleep. Her fur looked healthy and a glorious rich colour. Her foxy batteries were on recharge and, if she had moved any closer to my house, she would have been inside with Mew and Jem. I sat as still as I could so as not to disturb her and let myself be in the moment. Just two friends sitting side by side in the afternoon sunshine. I use the word magical a lot to describe my time with Vix because this truly was a magical moment.

This page: Vix sleeping ever closer.

Above: The eyes are the window of the soul.

Sometimes it felt as if Vix was just popping by to say 'Hello' and have a snack before going about her foxy business. It was no more than I expected from what I had been reading about foxes. Fluffy would have been about eighteen weeks old by then and finding food independently. Vix would slowly be returning to her pre-Mum fox life. She was out and about later in the day as if returning to a more crepuscular lifestyle. Despite her briefer daytime visits she was also beginning to show up later in the evening, often as late as 8.30pm. It was an ever-changing cycle still destined to keep me on my toes.

Above: Relaxing..

As I was once more clearing litter on my drive, a neighbour spotted me and we stood, the regulation two metres apart as had become the norm, chatting about the latest rules of social distancing, handwashing, sanitisers, and forming bubbles with family and friends. We talked about the things that helped us as we spent time at home. I mentioned Vix and she asked if my fox might have rabies. It was a stark reminder that not everyone was as knowledgeable about British wildlife and, more precisely, foxes, as I and my friends were. When something is your passion, and your parents taught you about nature and animals as you grew up, it is easy to forget that other people have a vastly different experience of the world around them. If no one points out a bird and tells you what it is called why would you know its name? Perhaps they view the natural world as little more than an inconvenience, dropping leaves on their car or well-manicured lawn, or, heaven help us their artificial turf.

My neighbour's comment made me worry for Vix. Did everyone around me consider her a danger? Did my neighbours think all foxes had rabies? That Vix would kill their cats and attack their children? I knew there had been stories of fox attacks in the United Kingdom, but the evidence was either not convincing or the reports appeared confusing. Fox bites were rare and considered less harmful than a bite from a cat. I felt compelled to do something. For the first time in my life, I planned to contact all my neighbours. Something about Vix was making me do things I had never done before. I was emboldened by my love of a wild animal. My concern for her well-being was pushing me beyond my comfort zone and stretching my, previously limited, boundaries.

I sat down at the computer and began to type. I produced a leaflet about Vix and other foxes. I included a couple of photographs and what I hoped was helpful information. I had a sense of purpose as I posted them through forty neighbours' letterboxes.

"Hello Neighbours,

I am Marion and we may have waved to each other when we clapped for the NHS.

A beautiful fox is visiting me in my garden. I have named her Vix and have treated her, with medication from the vet, for mange. She is a very gentle soul and is distinguishable as she has a scar below her left ear on her temple. She brought one cub to see me.

I want to make sure she will be all right through the coming months and help her all I can...She does cross the road, so *please take care when you are driving and if you see an injured fox, please let me know.*

Foxes in the UK do not have rabies.

Foxes will not harm your cats, you or pets unless they are cornered or frightened, when then they will defend themselves.

However, if you have outdoor rabbits, guinea pigs or chickens they need to be in fox-safe hutches.

Foxes will bury food and the occasional shoe in your garden just like dogs will.

I hope you will help me look after Vix.

Thank you for reading.

Marion"

I hoped my leaflet would help raise local awareness of foxes and improve their reputation. However, later that day when I returned from a shopping trip to Sainsbury's there was Vix standing on the roof of a neighbour's car, like the Monarch of the Glen. I pulled in quickly, wound my car window down and called out across the road: 'What are you doing up there? I'm trying to make people like you'. Vix gave me a squinty smile. Being an intelligent fox, she was making sure, from an excellent vantage point, that the road was clear before crossing, although I did not think paw marks on a neighbour's car roof were going to help our cause.

Above: Squinty smile in her spot.

Above: Vix, beautiful in profile.

As we entered the last half of July, Vix's behaviour and visits continued to change. When she popped by during the afternoon she would have a snack, as any of us would when calling in on a friend to say hello and chat. She often gave me a nose bump or licked my leg as her way of saying thank you before disappearing over the fence. When she returned later, which still seemed to be around 8.30pm, she was a proper fox again, sniffing the ground, ears erect, eyes ever watchful of the comings and goings in the garden and beyond. Perhaps the movement of other foxes was keeping her on her toes. Vix might eat a small piece of chicken, but she was not interested in anything more. It was as if the call of the wild was in action once dusk fell. She was a fox-on-a-mission and more skittish and alert. I did not know if this was normal behaviour at this point in the fox calendar. Maturing foxes from other families would be exploring each other's territories and that would surely put Vix on alert for Fluffy's safety as well as her own. There was an increasing number of people about, now that lockdown had eased and perhaps that was causing the change. It was interesting to compare Vix's behaviour with that of other foxes observed by members of the Self Isolating Bird Club.

Above: Vix, shows us her teeth..

With lockdown eased I was able to go out and meet friends I have known since University. We reunited at Hever Castle, Kent, once the home of Anne Boleyn, the second wife of Henry VIII. We met in the car park with cheerful waves and smiles and spent our visit outside walking and sitting, at a socially acceptable distance, in the magnificent gardens overlooking the lake. It was wonderful to see them again. We met when we were fresh-faced eighteen-year-olds, starting our university journey. We studied and revised together then graduated and travelled to New York and Iceland. Our conversation may have changed from the frivolities of youth to the colour of our curtains but they have been an amazing support to me through tough times and I love them dearly.

The problem with Covid-19 was that so many of us could have the virus, be passing it on to others and not know it. Being asymptomatic had become a household word and, even though some could not spell it, most people knew what it meant. We could not hug hello or goodbye, so spending the day outside was the sensible option. We had brought a picnic lunch so that we could eat and chat in the sunshine and settled, one at each corner of a bench, to protect each other.

Being with friends was a delightful treat. One benefit of lockdown for many of us was discovering what we really valued. When you were asked to stay indoors for long periods of time, the majority of people did not miss driving their fancy car or wearing designer clothes. They wanted to hug their family, see a new-born grandchild or chat with a friend. News reporters were constantly asking members of the public "What do you miss most?" and the majority of answers referred to seeing family or not being able to hug a loved one. It was things money could not buy, that we all now craved and I hope that long after the Covid crisis has passed we will remember what truly mattered.

The pandemic also highlighted who was valued by society. With a deadly virus sweeping the world we did not need overpaid music stars, talentless reality 'stars' or men who could kick a ball, we needed the hardworking hourly-paid cleaner, the bus and delivery drivers, the shelf-stacker at the supermarket and we needed nurses, doctors and scientists to save us. I hope the importance of these members of our society will not be forgotten and their wages will reflect their true value to us all.

At the end of my day out, I could not hug my friends goodbye and that was a hard thing to deal with. I missed that human contact. As I sat in the car ready to head home I found myself looking at my watch at Vix-time wondering what she would do when she arrived in my garden and did not find me there. Would she be alright? Obviously, she would. As much as I did not like the feeling, I thought it would be good for her to learn that there would be times when I would not be there. If she were still visiting when the summer holidays ended my teaching timetable would change. When the autumn and winter arrived, it would get dark earlier. Vix's own visiting times had already changed so we needed to learn a new routine going forward; to not always expect the other to be there.

It rained the next day and Vix sensibly found somewhere dry to stay, although sadly not in the shelter in my garden. She did not arrive at her usual time and that was understandable, but an hour later there was still no sign of her and I began to wonder if she would come at all. Had my absence caused this change? Had she already left to find a new territory? Although it was not supposed to be the time of year for that to happen, months are set by humans not by nature. Spring's arrival, marked by the appearance of daffodils or apple blossom, is earlier or later each year depending on the weather, so the fox calendar must surely react the same. I tried to go about my business and not keep looking out of the window. It was easier said than done and on one of my frequent checks I was delighted to see Vix sniffing around the pond. My worries were for nothing. My friend was back.

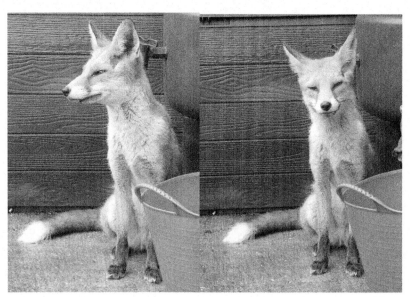

Above: Waiting for her human.

Unlike some of us who are always trying to lose weight the fact that Vix was filling out was a good sign. Foxes will hunt and feed on birds, rabbits, and rodents. They will also eat fruit, frogs, and worms. They seemed to enjoy digging up the bulbs in my garden and some discarded fish and chips or a piece of fried chicken will also go down well. Obviously Vix needed more calories when nursing and feeding her cubs but by the end of July between my garden and natures' bounty she no doubt had more than enough food, which explained why she could now afford to be picky about what she ate at Chez Marion. Foxes, apparently, need around 500kcal per day or 121kcal for every kg of body weight. I was not able to weigh Vix, although it gave me a smile imagining trying to do so.

"Get on the scales, Vix, please!"

"No." Squinty smile.

"I just want to weigh you."

"Don't be ridiculous."

Towards the end of July when Vix headed off, after having her fill of chompy-chicken, she paused at the top of the fence and gave me a long look and our eyes met. It was strangely poignant, and I felt something akin to foreboding. I hoped it was not goodbye but I had an overwhelming feeling that it was. I could not explain it and I am glad I posted the sentiment on the SIBC Facebook page because of what happened next. It was strangely prophetic.

Above: Vix excels at the beam.

Above: Vix tail has filled out.

Above: Enjoying some chompy chicken.

Above: Vix on a flower pot and in her spot.

There was no sign of Vix the next day, no clatter on the fence, no flash of ginger fur. It was extremely hot even for a summer's day and I hoped that she was somewhere safe, sheltering from the heat. No doubt she would have cached food to keep her going but I was concerned. That long look she had given me still troubled me. I sat out for as long as I could that night waiting, hoping, that she would be there, but she never came. Perhaps she would visit during the night and I left some food out just in case.

There was still no sign of Vix on the last day of July. It was strange to sit in the garden and not have her appear and give me that lovely slow blink and squinty smile. It made me sad and I felt the loss of her company and hollow without her.

I had been having sessions with a counsellor to help me work through my feelings of loss and grief since Brian's death. I constantly recalled walking with my husband to the chemotherapy department and watching nurses insert a picc line into the permanent port under his skin. I relived searching for a wheelchair for him, the endless walks along hospital corridors, the signs to oncology and intensive care. I was plagued by repeated images of nurses at his bedside taking his blood pressure or attending to a drip. I could so vividly recall his frail form beneath the blankets as he slept, and I was forever reliving the moment a doctor told me my husband 'could die tonight'. Even today the beeps of intensive care machines in the background of television news reports take me back to the hospital, to ICU, to A and E, to nurses and doctors, to boxes of gloves on the wall above the sink, to needles inserted under frail skin, to being positive, smiling and cheerful, to not letting Brian see how frightened I was for him, how terrified I was of losing him and how I was screaming inside. Perhaps it was Post Traumatic Stress rearing its head or just the normal cycle of grief, but it helped to air my feelings with someone trained to understand.

And now that Vix was missing, I felt bereft. Her visits had become fleeting, but I looked forward to them none the less. I knew she was healthier than she had been for many months but there was that awful thought that she had been hit by a car and lay somewhere injured or dead. I charged up the night camera batteries, inserted the microSD card, clicked the switch to 'on' and prayed I would to catch sight of her on that.

Above: A classic Vix pose.

AUGUST 2020

The Fox year- August

Foxes will now be most active between dusk and dawn. Berries become an important food source along with rodents. Cubs have grown considerably and will look more like the adults. Barks may be issued by the dog fox and vixen as they call to their offspring or warn them of danger.

Bees buzzed around the salvias, roses opened, and butterflies fed on the nectar filled purple buddleia flowers. The apples and pears began to swell promising a very small apple pie and a crunchy pear in weeks to come. I waited eagerly for the tomatoes to ripen and the newer plants I had added to the garden to reveal their potential.

When August arrived Vix had stopped visiting and I was worried. There was no sign of her on the night camera although it did capture another fox and I wondered if it was Fluffy. The fox looked young and from the square face shape I deduced it was male. Of course, when it turned around and gave me a full view of his testicles, there was no question as to his gender. Was Vix keeping away from my garden to allow Fluffy to explore his new world? I wish I knew. I just wanted to know she was safe.

On a trip to the supermarket, I decided to drive around the side streets looking for any sign of Vix. I drove slowly, casting glances at the kerb close to my home, in case the body of a fox lay there. I realise that makes me sound like a kerb-crawler, but it was a different foxy lady I was looking for. Cars are the biggest killers of our urban foxes. Fortunately, there was no body in the gutter but also no sign of Vix. However, as I drove passed the church a young fox dashed along the hedge and disappeared through the foliage into the vicarage garden. I was sure it was Fluffy. I stopped the car, got out and peered through the hedge to see if I could spot where Fluffy had gone, but alas he was no longer visible. It was good to have had a sighting of Fluffy but there was still no news of Vix. I headed off to purchase my essential shopping.

It was a sad fact that I had come to rely on Vix being there; her visits brought me pleasure, gave me focus and took me away from the feelings of despair I often felt. She was a comfort to me and brightened my days. I was emotionally involved with my foxy friend, and it felt odd to be out in the garden and not see her. I am not ashamed to say I had a good cry. My emotions were never too far from the surface since Brian died. I could be fine for days and then something small would have me sobbing my heart out. All of the energy would be sapped from me, and I was overwhelmed once more. I sat crying at the news reports of deaths from Covid-19, I crumpled into a heap on the kitchen floor when I accidentally dropped something and balled my eyes out when I found a piece of paper with Brian's writing on it or an object that brought back a memory of things I would never do again. Mew would wander over to me and stand with a confused look on her face, as water fell from my eyes. If Jem was alone with me when I began to emit body-wracking sobs she would run out of the room, returning a few moments later with her mum at her side. I could almost imagine the conversation that brought Mew in to see me.

"Mum, she's crying again. What should I do?"

"Leave it to me," Mew would reply.

Mew would nuzzle me or give me a nose bump sensing my distress. I could not love her more than I do. Mew and Jem are my companions, and my family. After a good cry, I picked myself up, dried my tears and got on with whatever task I was involved with before the tears fell. There was no one else to do things for me, so I had to face whatever lay ahead. I had told Brian never to give up and it was time to take my own advice. I still had his house to empty and sell but with travel restricted there was only so much I could do.

The news was filled quite rightly with Coronavirus. Families were unable to be with their loved ones as they died in a care home or hooked up to machines in intensive care. It was happening more and more all over the World; the number of deaths was continuing to rise. Employees were on reduced income, businesses were closing or would soon be bankrupt. Washing your hands, wearing a mask, keeping a safe distance between friends had become the norm.

And on the flip side the natural world was recovering. With less traffic on the roads, less footfall in the parks, less noise, less air traffic, less pollution, nature seemed to utter a sigh of relief. The sky seemed bluer. In spring we heard the birds more clearly and people were looking and listening, maybe for the first time, at the world around them; at the world close to home. Having a garden proved to be a boon but even a window box could provide a glimpse of wildlife, with a colourful flower encouraging a visit from a bee. I needed my garden and the solace it brought even more in 2020.

And then Vix was back. I was overjoyed to look out of the window and see my foxy friend sniffing at the flowers and walking through the plants. However, I sensed something was wrong, her demeanor had changed. Vix was injured.

Vix's left ear was torn, some of the skin was hanging off and there was dried blood on the fur of her head. I assumed she had been involved in a fight but, whether with a cat, dog, or another fox there seemed no way to tell. Vix was subdued and wary. The light in her eyes had gone out. Her eyes were downcast, and her shoulders drooped. It was heartbreaking to see the change in her demeanor. She came towards me, and I spoke gently, hoping to reassure her. There was fear in her eyes and uncertainty. I offered a gentle voice, something familiar to eat and a safe place to rest.

I could only hope that, as she was now physically healthier, Vix's immune system would also be stronger, and she would be able to fight off any infection that might take hold where the skin had been broken and torn. If the fight had been over territory, was it over? Would she return with more injuries and if so, was there anything I could do to treat the wounds or speed her recovery? That night when she left, she took a piece of my heart with her. I headed to the internet to investigate if there was anything I could add to her food to help to ward off infection or to act as pain relief.

Above: Squinting in the sunshine.

Research suggested I could give Vix honey to help the healing process. The next day, I grabbed my car keys and headed to the supermarket to buy honey for a fox. Despite the Covid rules I was sure everyone would agree it was essential travel.

Manuka honey, in fact honey in general, is renowned for its antibacterial properties. Manuka honey is produced by bees in Australia and New Zealand from the nectar of the manuka tree and its rarity seems to govern the price. Medical grade honeys have antibacterial properties against bacteria known to show resistance to antibiotics and as such offer treatment when conventional medicines fail. However, at just under £10 a jar it was the most expensive honey I had ever bought, and I had bought it for a fox, albeit an incredibly special one.

Once home I smeared pieces of chicken with the honey and waited for Vix to appear. Later that day, when she climbed over the fence and descended into my garden, she was still subdued, but the wound had completely dried. At least that meant no further entry point for infection; hooray for platelets and the clotting process. I chatted to Vix, explained what I had been up to and offered her the honey-smeared chompy-chicken. She would eat it and be cured! Vix however, gave the honeyed chicken only a few licks before declaring it undesirable. So much for foxes finding sweet things irresistible. No one had told Vix that. It seemed I would be having expensive honey on my porridge for a while.

Wanting to be sure I had done all I could for Vix I contacted the South Essex Wildlife Hospital and they informed me that ear flap wounds usually heal themselves. This was good news. However, I sent some photographs of Vix's ear to them so that they could confirm the diagnosis and get back to me if they felt I needed to do anymore. Fortunately, I did not. Time was once again to prove the healer but in the meantime my friend's confidence had taken a battering.

Above: Vix, such a beautiful red fox.

Seeing Vix hurt and subdued reminded me yet again just how precarious a fox's life is. Although red foxes can easily live for nine years, in urban areas in the United Kingdom, the average life span is just eighteen months. Most urban fox deaths are due to road traffic accidents. I had no idea how old Vix was, so no way of knowing where she was on that perilous eighteen-month timeline. I had only a vague idea where she went and what dangers she might face. I knew she had to cross a main road and that the fields were used frequently by dog walkers. Was her injury due to an intraspecific fight or had a dog attacked her, cornered her or, worse still, had a dog been deliberately set upon her? Not everyone is as enamoured by foxes as my friends in the SIBC.

Despite hunting with dogs being banned in the England and Wales by the Hunting Act in 2005 (it was banned in Scotland in 2002) foxes are still deliberately killed. Trail hunting is legal and involves urine and carcasses being used to lay a scent trail for the dogs to follow. The fear is that in doing so they may flush out and follow a live animal instead. There are still Hunts, there are still red-coated riders galloping across the countryside to the blast of a horn rallying the dogs and a terrified animal runs for its life. The pro-hunting lobby will speak of the destruction of a way of life and British culture. We used to burn women at the stake and call them witches, but times have thankfully changed, and we no longer hold on to that part of 'British culture'. We can no longer justify terrifying another living creature because some people think it's fun.

The thought of anyone deliberately hurting Vix summoned all my maternal instincts to protect her, but unlike Mew, I could not bring her into my home.

The sadness in Vix's eyes told me the hurt was not just physical. Whatever the cause of her injuries, it had clearly frightened her. Vix had lost some of her confidence; her cheekiness had gone, and she was content just to shelter in a corner of the garden, her back against one of my garden boxes where nothing could sneak up on her.

Vix was still nervous and skittish the following day. She ate some chicken as she sat with me and then took some away. Later, when I looked out into the garden she was back in her spot, curled up, nose tucked under her tail, but eyes still alert. It was her safe place. I went outside, talked gently to her, and settled down on the bench. I informed her I would sit with her, that she was safe and could relax because I would be there keeping watch again. Vix seemed to understand because as I sat reading, she slept. We were together in the garden for about an hour, her fur rising and falling in slumber. Once again I was humbled by the fact that she trusted me and that I could return the joy she had given me by protecting her and providing a sanctuary. When she awoke, Vix stretched her legs out in front of her, arched her back and yawned contentedly. She gave me a squinty smile and a look that suggested she was ready for something to eat. I gave her an egg and some cat food which she ate before heading off over the fence.

Vix's injured ear.

"How's your fox?" people would ask, and she was *my* fox. Not in terms of ownership or possession but because I could identify her, and she was singled out from all the others. I knew this fox, I knew her personality, I knew the feel of her wet nose and, when we met, we smiled at each other.

I warned the students I taught via Skype, that I would have to leave for a few minutes should 'my injured fox' appear during a lesson. Fortunately, they knew me well enough to understand how soft I was about Vix. I taught for over 20 years in a Mainstream school, and I no longer feel the need to be 'Miss' with my students when I can now be, Marion. I want the people I teach to feel relaxed and safe enough to admit when they do not understand something, then the learning process is so much easier. Having a giggle as you learn always helps and what better way to relax than with talk of a friendly fox.

Vix did turn up mid-lesson as predicted and I went outside with an egg, cat food and chicken. They say the eyes are the windows of the soul and I could tell from the brightness in Vix's eyes, that she was feeling better. She was more alert, both ears were standing up and although she was not back to her relaxed self, there was a definite improvement in her demeanor. Vix was on the mend both physically and mentally. I returned to the laptop to impart the good news to my student. It was not just the members of the SIBC who were following Vix's progress and anxious for her safety.

As the mid-August temperatures continued to climb and the humidity rose in Southern England, the Fox Pool went out again for any animal wanting to cool its paws which seemed to be mostly me. I pottered in the house or garden and then, as the temperatures soared and my face turned pink from the heat, I would go for a blood cooling paddle. Tux lay in the shade, sheltering from the heat of the day, the tip of his tail giving the occasional flick of irritation as a fly landed on him. Indoors, the sun's rays streaming in through the French windows cast areas of warmth on the carpet and Jem and Mew took up a position in the warm beams.

The sparrows had turned the tranquil solar fountain into a bird spa. Water splashed everywhere as six of them flapped their wings frantically as they bathed. Each would emerge soaked through, bedraggled, and looking like the proverbial drowned rat. I was astonished they were able to fly to a nearby tree but once there they took their time drying off and rearranging their feathers. When the starlings arrived the noise level rose as they squawked and battled for the best spot in the water. Their long beaks could be used as weapons should anyone not make enough room.

Vix delayed her visit until the early evening when it turned cooler. I did not blame her for sheltering during the heat of the day. After she had eaten, she settled into her spot for a rest. Whatever was happening in the fox world, it seemed the dispute with Vix was over, at least for now. Was she the victor or the victim? It was impossible to tell. There was more fox activity on the night camera, and I was sure I had identified four different foxes. I assumed one was Fluffy and could identify another male fox but who were the others; this year's young cubs beginning to explore their world or older foxes edged out of their territories by the new brood? It would be interesting to see how my visitors changed in the months ahead.

Monday 10th August 2020

One year ago, today, Brian, my boyfriend of twenty-eight years, said "Come on, let's do this properly" and got down on one knee and asked me to marry him. I wish he were here to share that wonderful memory with me.

It is true that the first year after someone dies is the hardest. You face a year of firsts. I had already endured the first Christmas and Brian's birthday without him. The 10th August was the day we officially became engaged and yet one year later I was alone. For most couples it becomes a part of their life; a day to celebrate, to reminisce about who proposed to whom, and where the proposal took place. Was it romantic? Was it a surprise? Now it will always be tinged with sadness. I filled the day with activity trying to keep my mind off the sorrow I felt but it crept back in weighing down my heart. I cuddled with Mew and Jem, before heading off to Brian's house for some more sorting. Every visit there was filled with memories. I could envisage him sitting in his chair, making us both a cup of tea, watering plants in the garden or greeting me at the front door. The house was filled with ghosts. Not sheet wearing Scooby-Doo ones but, if I stood still, in the corner of the room, I could almost watch the memories play out before my eyes. After a couple of hours, I headed home, at one point slowing down for a group of Indian Runner ducks that were standing at the side of the road. It was only as I drew closer that I realised they were in fact a group of abandoned empty wine bottles. Google them and you will see it was an easy mistake. Membership of the Self Isolating Bird Club was influencing me. I was seeing birds everywhere and it brought a smile on an otherwise sad day.

I have always loved foxes. Basil Brush, the puppet fox, was one of my childhood heroes, especially in his programme with 'Mister Derek', the late actor, Derek Fowlds. After so many years I was a fox fan again. Books on foxes dropping through my letter box had become a regular occurrence. I researched their life cycle, their feeding, and more. It was therefore a real shock to read that the retail giant Amazon sold fox snares. Snares are a thin piece of wire shaped into a noose. When an animal runs through them the wire tightens, usually lassoing them about the neck, trapping them. As they attempt to escape the animal may further injure itself. If the person who set the snare, usually a game keeper, does not check the snare regularly, who knows how long the animal may remain trapped and suffering. It may die of dehydration, exhaustion or be killed by a predator. Snares cannot discriminate. They may trap your dog or cat as easily as the animal they are set for. And yes, they are legal in the United Kingdom. I sent a message to Amazon asking why they were selling animal snares and if this was something they really wanted to be associated with. I received an email informing me that the snares were placed on their site by a third party, and they would be contacting them for further information. I sent the same message months later when I noticed the snares were still for sale. At the time of writing in 2021, I have heard no more, and they are still for sale. Leafletting neighbours, questioning global conglomerates, one small fox was having a huge influence on me.

As the scorching summer continued, I kept the chompy-chicken and eggs in the fridge to provide a cool snack for Vix. She continued to pop by during the day or early in the evening, sometimes she would stay to eat and at other times she would grab a bite 'to go'. She would appear on top of the fence or strolling down the garden and give me her characteristic blink and squinty smile to say hello.

Above: Vix curls her tongue.

Knowing Vix's new routine, I found myself looking at the clock and muttering to myself 'Oh, I had better get Vix's chicken ready," much to the distain of my cats. At times I would get the food ready, step out into the garden and find her there. We were becoming spookily in sync. In wet weather Vix often turned up looking dry so it was good to know she had somewhere to shelter even if she had not taken advantage of the 'new build' shelter at the bottom of my garden. On other occasions she turned up soaked through.

When Vix failed to appear one night I was not worried. She had missed days on previous occasions and still returned. There was no reason to think she would not do so again, although I admit the thought of her being hit by a car on the busy main road remained a constant worry and the possibility of another ear-injuring fight was also a concern. However, I knew she was finding food elsewhere, knew she had a dry place to shelter and was strong enough to fend for herself.

Above: Waiting patiently again.

However, when Vix returned she was injured once more. Vix was limping on her left back paw. It was swollen and she was avoiding putting weight on it. Vix had arrived limping on a previous occasion, before we really knew each other, and she was back to her old self within a day or two, so I hoped this was just a sprain and that it too would heal. Vix could climb the fence and despite the discomfort, could still use her foot. I would monitor the situation and if intervention became necessary, I had a selection of telephone numbers for wildlife hospitals at my disposal.

And the next day...her paw was so much better. The ability to recover quickly from an injury is a selective advantage for all wild animals and fortunately it was working for Vix. If it had been many people I know, they would have enjoyed complaining about it for weeks to come.

Above: Vix, was a stunningly beautiful fox.

Just when I thought our routine was set in stone Vix began to arrive earlier and I wondered if it was a way to avoid other foxes. Perhaps the injury to her foot was not just the result of a badly timed jump but due to an encounter with another fox. Whatever the reason and whenever she chose to visit, it was fine by me.

Like many members of the Self Isolating Bird Club, I tried my hand at various art forms during lockdown. Some had picked up their watercolour paints again whilst others dusted off their pencils. One or two members finally had the courage to post their work on an internet page filled with kind and encouraging people. Flowers and petals were arranged, and photos shared. Wood was sculpted, stones were painted and felt was stabbed, yes stabbed. The Facebook page was alive with amazing paintings, drawings, and all kinds of creations. One craft that caught my eye was needle felting. I was not sure how you could turn felt into amazingly detailed tiny animals but, if you will pardon the pun, I felt the urge to have a go. I sent away for a kit. Sending away for things had also become the new norm in a world where going to the shops for non-essential items was either discouraged or no longer possible. The kit arrived. I was going to make a felt fox, it seemed appropriate.

My first attempt did not look a great deal like the picture on the box and I posted a photo of it for the SIBC to see. Their advice to 'keep stabbing the fox', although somewhat alarming, proved invaluable. It seems that with needle felt the more you stab your creation, the more it takes the desired form. I imagine part of the attraction of needle-felting is the opportunity to take out your anger on some innocent felt. However, I am not sure Vix would have approved of either my final piece or the 'keep stabbing the fox' advice.

Along with clearing and sorting my husband's possessions I had also become the owner of his car. Two cars now sat on my drive, Brian's Suzuki, and my beloved, but elderly, Ford Fiesta, Ralph. My family have always named their cars. When my Dad proudly arrived home with a blue Mini Cooper in the 1960s, we called it Bluey. When I think of sitting in the back of Bluey with my Mum and a pile of cuddly toys 'the family' at my side, it seemed so spacious. Such is the view of the world from the eyes of a five-year-old. Over the years there was Angie the Anglia, Yarna the Ford Escort along with many others. My own first car was a Fiat 126 I named Lollipop. She was a car with a very unique character, unable to overtake a milk float if it was going uphill and refusing to start if it had been raining the night before but I loved her. Ralph was the first car I owned with electric windows. Oh, the joy of pressing a button instead of using a winding handle. Ralph took my Mum and I on many trips out to the countryside to witness the changing seasons. We stopped by a field to look at the lambs or drove along country lanes lined with trees in their autumn colours and Mum reminisced about the avenue of trees at Rickmansworth school where she was evacuated during the Second World War. When Mum required care and was going to stay with my brother, for respite, we arranged a 'hostage exchange' at Reading services on the M4. Ralph never complained as the miles piled up. When Brian was in hospital I drove to and from the hospital every day, clocking up over 400 miles in a week. As Brian received treatment for cancer Ralph began to struggle with all I asked of him. Three times he broke down but always in a place of safety. Once in the village next to Brian's allowing me to still reach him on foot, once outside his house and the third time on an off ramp of a dual carriageway, where I was found by the police who kindly towed my car to a nearby garage. I took each breakdown in my stride because Brian's struggle for life put everything else in perspective. When I inherited Brian's younger car, I knew it was time to let Ralph go but it was a wrench handing over the keys to another person and walking away. It was yet another loss I faced alone, and it broke my heart. How much more battering could I take?

I decided I needed to go out, out. Not just take a trip to the shops for essentials but to visit places again and to meet, with social distanced, friends. I was going to go 'proper out'. I needed a change of scenery to lift my mood. Having checked the weather forecast, I took myself off to the seaside, getting up at the crack of dawn to drive to the beach so that I could sit on the pebbles just after sunrise and listen to the waves lapping gently on the shore. The sea air lifted my spirits as did the gulls calling overhead. All that was missing was a bag of chips, the smell of salt and vinegar assaulting my nose. It is a well-known fact that chips taste best when eaten as you walk along the sea front. Unfortunately, I did not have any chips, but you cannot have everything.

After a while I drove along the coast to a sandy beach. The car park at that time of the morning was almost empty. I parked, took off my shoes and socks and headed to the beach for a proper British paddle, splashing in the waves as I wandered along beachcombing. Shells of cockles and mussels were interspersed with those of Tellins, which are also small bivalve molluscs, and have bands of different colours on their shells. All the names from my marine ecology courses came back to me as

I strolled and dropped to the ground every now and then to pick up and examine a treasure. As other people started to arrive, I headed back to the car, the sand still stuck to my feet. It had a been a safe, coronavirus free trip and I arrived home with a smile on my face and sand in my socks and between my toes. Nature had boosted me yet again.

On another occasion I met a friend at the Hawk Conservancy Trust near Andover, Hampshire. It had been mentioned and recommended by Chris Packham during one of the SIBC broadcasts. I had never been to the Trust before and I was impressed by the large well-kept aviaries and their obvious passion for the work they do. The wind and rain of recent days held off allowing the flying displays to go ahead. I came away with a new appreciation for birds of prey and discovered a particular fondness for vultures. It had also been nice to share the experience with a friend and to sit and eat a meal that I had not had to cook for myself. Simple pleasures rediscovered in times of crisis.

As well as enjoying my posts about Vix and following her journey I was delighted by the number of people on the SIBC, who had drawn, painted, or created something inspired by her. I was amazed at the talent people had. Vix was bringing me huge enjoyment but she was also giving others pleasure too. I had shared a few photographs of a sickly fox and it had evolved into so much more, spreading happiness to so many and I find that wonderful; the knock-on effect Vix's presence created. One of the first artists to capture Vix for me was Alison Paterson. She sent me a photo of a watercolour of Vix sitting beside one of my blue painted flowerpots, pots that it seems had become 'celebrities' too. It is beautiful and hangs on my wall as I type. Another artist who asked to draw Vix was Kathryn Coyle. I did not know it at the time but Kathryn and I would end up collaborating on a children's book about Vix, the Lockdown Fox.

Despite the heat Vix never did paddle in the fox pool. She took a drink from it but when full of water she did not step in. However, one afternoon, after a snooze to fight off a migraine I looked out into the garden and saw Vix smiling back at me. She was sitting in the fox pool which no longer had any water in it. She looked adorable and it has become an iconic picture of her. I saw her sitting in the empty pool several times, but none were as memorable as the first. I am so glad I managed to snap a photograph.

Having spotted Vix in the pool I went outside to offer her a chicken drumstick. Usually, she will signal her desire for it with a lick of her lips or she would sit down to let me know I may place it on the ground for her, but that day she stepped forward, sniffed it, and took the chicken from my hand. It was never my intention to feed her by hand; never my intention to encourage her to approach people for food but it was an incredible thrill. As for allowing her to do so, I had taken a migraine tablet, so I blame the drugs.

Above: Vix in the pet pool.

As August drew to a close, there was an autumnal nip in the air. Gone were the days of standing in the fox pool to cool down. Now I sat in the garden wearing a jacket and wrapping my hands around a warm cup of tea. Vix appeared over the fence and dropped down into the garden via the fox shelter roof. It was proving useful after all if not for the intended purpose. Vix's coat was beginning to fill out and her tail, once so sad and thin was now fluffy and white tipped. She took a piece of chicken from me and buried it in one of my flowerpots. Perhaps the change in temperature had triggered a 'cache it for winter' signal in her brain. It was nice to have Vix stick around for a while longer and it reminded me of the days when she would find a comfortable place to sleep as I sat reading.

On the penultimate day of August, I visited the British Wildlife Centre at Lingfield, Surrey. It was another organisation recommended by Chris Packham and Megan McCubbin in the Self Isolating Bird Club broadcasts. Emboldened by membership of the SIBC I made a video of my trip and posted it on the Facebook page. I wanted to show others what the Centre was like and help them to decide if it was worth a visit. The Centre is home to many different British wild animals and is involved in various captive breeding and release programmes. During the week they welcome school parties, educating children about the wildlife around them. I loved my day there. When the keepers give a talk, they enter the enclosures and, knowing that this means food is available, the animals miraculously appear from the bushes you have previously been scouring for a sign of the occupant. This gives you a greater opportunity to observe the animals and take photographs. I snapped happily away with my camera and was particularly entranced by Flo and Basil, two of the foxes, and the wildcat kittens. On discovering they also offered Photography days I knew I would be signing up for one and making a return visit to the Centre. Since then I have attended three photography days and met several SIBC members there.

Above: Vix looking fit and fabulous.

September 2020

The Fox year- September

The cubs will now be harder to distinguish from the adults, being almost fully grown. Dispersal of this year's youngsters begins as they seek new territories away from their parents.

With the arrival of September, I was back to teaching in school, face to face with actual three-dimensional people. There was hand sanitizer in the hallway, the tables were further apart and constantly cleaned, and the staff wore masks as they moved about the building. 'Bubbles' were created such that students stayed with a particular group all day. Groups were small enough to allow social distancing. Precautions were taken but there was no guarantee we would be able to keep each other safe. Grandparents may easily have been infected by school children taking the virus home, and teachers were more likely to suffer from the virus than the children they taught. Teachers were risking their health to educate the nation's children, to allow parents to go to work and to keep the country's economy functioning. However, it was nice to interact with actual people and not just a face on a computer screen.

As my routine altered Vix's visits changed yet again. Sometimes we would miss each other entirely, or I would catch a quick glimpse of her increasingly bushy tail as she jumped over the fence. Once I saw her disappearing into a hedge on the other side of the road. On other occasions she would arrive early and catch me by surprise although never unprepared. Her food was always ready. Cutting up chompy-chicken and storing it in a box in the fridge was still part of my daily routine. There was a comfortable familiarity about time with Vix.

I loved being a member of the Self Isolating Bird Club so much that I suggested when Lockdown was over, when we had all been vaccinated, could travel freely and could meet again, that we hold a SIBC Murmuration. It was a genuine desire to gather these lovely people together and for us to finally meet. I envisaged it as a Great British Fair, the sort of thing that brought back memories from childhood with a coconut shy, tombola and cake stalls.   Ladies in pinny's selling Victoria sponge cakes, children nagging their parents for money to buy an ice cream and Dad's showing their lack of throwing prowess by failing to knock a hairy nut off a metre-high cup. The idea of flocking together in the manner of starlings went down well. The SIBC members joined in the fun volunteering to bake cakes, lemon drizzle being the favourite, make bunting (another wonderful bird reference) and wanting to 'gently reference' their favourite bird or animal in the manner of SIBC member and artist, Paul Harfleet. It would be a joyous event and an idea of hope for a brighter future. I hope the Murmuration occurs one day. We grow ever closer to it becoming a reality.

Above: Vix, in profile.

I had decreased my working hours during Brian's cancer treatment and reduced them further following his death. Life has different priorities now and I could not be bothered with the everyday. This meant that despite the start of the autumn term I still had days when I could spend time in the garden painting stones blue. It was an extension of my flowerpot painting and once the stones were blue, I decorated them with images like those on my flowerpots, cats, turtles, and a rainbow for the National Health Service. I placed them around the pond to add a little more colour to the garden. One afternoon, I had just finished painting, when Vix came by. She gave me a lovely squinty-eyed smile, which I continued to find adorable. As Hunter was in her way, she wandered through the flowerpots to get to her favourite place and ask what was on the menu. Chicken and egg was of course her 'usual' and that day she had egg, cat food and lots of chompy chicken. I was sniffed and received a wet nose bump. I took the opportunity to remind her about the large shelter at the bottom of the garden and how nice and snug it would be during the winter months. Her coat was filling out and she was now a wonderful mass of orange gorgeousness. I was not sure if she was paying much attention to what I said as she was lapping up the egg at the time. However, I reminded her that my garden was a safe place to be, there was ample room for a fox to overwinter and it meant she would not need to cross that dangerous road. I hoped she would mull it over.

Vix's ability to predict the weather fascinated me. On more than one occasion it would begin to rain not long after she had gone. Yes, I knew it was cloudy but how did she know it was going to rain so close to her visit? Could she smell it in the air? Detect a change in air pressure? Whatever it was she was better at forecasting the weather than I was.

"Why have you turned up at this time?" I would ask if she arrived early.

There would be no explanation but, a few minutes after Vix disappeared over the fence, the rain would begin to fall and all would become clear.

As September continued, the rush-hour traffic seemed to have returned to normal. The sound of cars zooming up and down the road at alarming speeds echoed off the houses and exacerbated my worry for Vix's safety. I knew she was aware of the dangers of the road and had seen her crossing it on several occasions, each time waiting sensibly for a gap in the traffic, but it was still a constant danger. The majority of fox deaths in urban areas are caused by vehicles.

Vix was now making two visits to my garden each day. The first would be in the early evening for her egg and a few bits of chicken. She would eat her fill and then head off over the fence with food in her mouth. She was still a fox on a mission with places to go. Vix was always more relaxed on her second visit, possibly because the search for food was no longer a priority. She had a full stomach so was able to take her time, or perhaps other foxes were no longer nearby, and she did not have to remain on guard. Whatever the reason, as the light was changing with the season, I knew her routine would too. I could only watch and wait for her arrival and provide whatever help I could.

Vix picked up another tick. At first, I thought it was a grass seed as she would often arrive adorned with them but as soon as the familiar white egg shape appeared, I knew a tick was growing behind her ear. I hoped that once again when the parasite had gorged its fill of blood it would fall off. Yet again the urge to remove it for her was strong as was the desire to brush her coat and give her fur a stroke. How I would have loved to make physical contact with her, but she was a wild animal who had simply chosen to befriend me, and I was playing my part by letting her be. However, as I placed the cat food down for her I felt Vix's teeth gently touch my finger. I was careful not to react, as snatching my hand away might have startled her. Vix had gently touched me with her teeth, possibly exploring to find out more about me and I was fine with that. She was always gentle with me and I never found anything threatening in her behaviour.

Above: My beautiful friend, Vix.

I wondered what a fox's memory is like. Does it compare to a dog's or a cat's? Did Vix recognise my face, my voice, my smell or am I a combination of several factors that identify me? I know my cats recognise me but would Vix know me in another context or does she associate me with my garden? Garden + Lady = Food? Would she need constant reinforcement that the garden was a safe place, and I was a person to trust or would she remember that no matter how much time passed? Many people have written about an animal returning after years and still looking for the person in the house who used to feed them, so I hope it will be the same with Vix and that she will remember me. Perhaps having a quick touch of my skin with her teeth helped fix me in her memory by adding additional information. There were so many unanswered questions. I hoped she would visit long enough for us to answer them together.

The natural world had proved to be a saviour for so many during lockdown and I was determined to see more of it once travel was possible. I had already visited two wildlife centres, new to me, in

August and in September I took a trip to another one. I got up early and drove to Wildwood near Herne Bay in Kent. My main aim in visiting was to see to animals I had a particular fondness for, a European Bison and an Elk, which were as close to an American Bison and a Moose as I could get. I decided to make another video to share with the SIBC. Wildwood is set in ancient woodland, the enclosures are large, and the animals in their care had plenty of room to roam around. Like so many places you now had to book your visit online in advance. On arrival we queued to be admitted and to either scan the NHS Test and Trace app on our phones or to leave our details so that if anyone was discovered to be positive for Covid we would be alerted and asked to self-isolate. Once inside I wandered along the paths, keeping socially distanced from other visitors. The beautiful Artic foxes drew my attention, I think we all know why. I made a mental note to return later in the year when their coats would have changed colour for winter, assuming they would do that in Kent. I chatted with a wild boar, met the Bison who plodded out of his stall for a walk about. I spotted the velvet as it peeled off the bleeding antlers of a reindeer and watched the pack of wolves padding along their well-worn paths within their enclosure. Despite many trips to Canada, including driving on roads adorned with signs warning you that moose were about, I had never seen a moose in the wild. The only one I had seen up until that point was sitting sullenly in Toronto zoo. The Elk at Wildwood, named Caramel, was also sitting down and showed little desire to get up for a moosey frolic. Perhaps I will see those long legs another day.

The newest attractions at Wildwood at that time were two bear cubs, Mish and Lucy. The adult bears had a wonderful space to roam and I watched as they searched for food hidden around their enclosure, using their long claws to turn over stones. The cubs next door were a cuddly delight. I knew by the end of my visit that I would return to spend more time with all the wonderful animals and I have been back to attend a photography day.

With an increase in the number of students, I began teaching later in the day, and there were yet more days when Vix and I did not see each other. I began to leave an egg, in the new bowl

I had bought for her, and often arrived home to find it gone. Either that or my neighbour would report that she had seen Vix and given her a piece of chicken. I had tried to explain to Vix that even if I am not there, food would be provided. My neighbour offered to put some out for Vix and I bagged up some pieces of chompy-chicken for her to have on standby. Apparently, Vix would look for me when she arrived in my garden and if I were still at work she would wait for a while, in case I appeared, then my neighbour kindly gave Vix some chicken and that seemed to be acceptable. I was pleased they had made a connection because I was preparing Vix and myself for a brief time apart. I planned to visit Scotland and wanted Vix to know that even if we did not see each other every day I would be back.

My first wedding anniversary was approaching, and I wanted to honour my husband by visiting places that meant so much to him and had happy memories for us both. It was the first 'holiday' I had ever taken on my own. I was not sure if it was a wise thing to do, knowing that it could bring forth many sad memories as it conjured up images of trips gone by. I was not sure if I would be emotionally strong enough or if returning to an empty hotel room at the end of the day was advisable. How would I face being overwhelmed by grief with neither Mew nor Jem there to offer a paw of comfort? Was being alone whilst combating depression and grief wise? Despite my reservations, I needed to make the trip. I wanted to go for Brian and to prove to myself that I could. Having had to cancel the same trip in April, when the first major Lockdown was put in place, now was the time to go. A friend would be feeding Mew and Jem and my neighbour was all set to feed Vix. There was nothing to stop me.

I flew to Inverness, wearing my face mask throughout my time at the departure airport and on the flight as was now the requirement. We might be freer to travel but Covid-19 had not gone away. I collected a hire car at Inverness Airport and drove to Culloden, scene of the infamous battle. On 16th April 1746, the last hand-to-hand battle on British soil took place between the Duke of Cumberland's government troops and Jacobite supporters of Charles Edward Stuart (Bonnie Prince Charlie), on Drummossie Moor, near Inverness, in the Scottish Highlands. Brian and I had been there many times and his name is on the ceiling of the visitor centre as one of the original contributors to its construction. I wanted to see Brian's name and was relieved to discover that the visitor's centre would be open when I arrived. Despite it being September in Scotland, the weather was balmy, and I walked in a t-shirt around the battlefield. I made my way to the Donald Stone, placed on the moor as a memorial to members of the MacDonald Clan who died in the battle, and sat for a while on a nearby bench talking to Brian. I wore a locket, bought for me by my brother, which contains a photograph of Brian and a lock of his hair. I told Brian I had brought him back to Culloden and that he would not believe I was sitting there in a t-shirt. I think he would have liked that. I found his name on the ceiling and stood for a moment remembering our last time visiting together.

From Culloden I drove alongside Loch Ness, the water calm enough to reflect the surrounding mountains. When you visit Scotland, you should be prepared for any weather and in September I had brought a small case packed with waterproofs and warm clothing, although on that day, it was not needed. I stopped and walked down to the Loch and put my hand in the cold water. It was a tranquil moment as the clouds moved slowly across the top of the mountains. There is something profoundly good for the soul about looking at mountains, listening to the leaves rustling on the branches and watching as the wind blows ripples across the water. It is the type of scenery Brian and I enjoyed holidaying in for many years. Scotland, Austria, and the west coast of Canada all have trees, mountains and vast bodies of water and they have called us back time and again. I spent that first night at the Premier Inn in Fort William. The room was clean, the staff wore face masks and at dinner we were all socially distanced. It was strange but it had become the norm to see people scattered around the restaurant with empty tables in between. I was impressed by all the hotel staff were doing to keep us safe and as an added bonus the bed and pillows were extremely comfortable and I slept well.

The next day, fully refreshed, I drove to Glencoe. As a McDonald, Brian felt a particular connection to the Coe and the Massacre that took place there on 13th February 1692. It is a particularly heinous tale of soldiers turning on the families who had given them food and shelter at the behest of Lord Stair. The massacre was carried out by a company commanded by Robert Campbell and the feud between the families is now a famous one. In solidarity with his ancestors Brian would never eat Campbell's soup; the Scots have a long memory. On the morning of my visit the skies were grey as I drove through the Glen and stopped in a lay-by to gaze upon the Three Sisters mountains, Beinn Fhada, Gearr Aonach and Aonach Dubh. I recalled when Brian paid a piper, in that very lay-by, to play a lament for the McDonalds and we watched clouds slide across the mountains as the sound of the bagpipes echoed through the Coe. Further along the glen I stopped at a small burn where Brian had always parked the car and I sat for a while, on a rock, listening to the water trickling over the stones, lost in my thoughts and memories. It was beautiful but someone was missing, Brian should have been there with me.

I found my way to the newly renovated Kingshouse Hotel, as it had been recommended to me by my brother as having spectacular views. However, my increasingly urgent mission by that point was to find a loo. To my delight as I pulled into the car park a mother red deer and her fawn wandered across the drive, soon to be followed by three more mothers and their offspring. They were beautiful animals with large brown eyes and delicate black hooves. I cannot fathom how anyone would gain pleasure from joining a shoot to kill them.

By the time I left the hotel, I had availed myself of their facilities, seen the fabulous view of the mountains from the hotel dining room, it was absolutely stunning, and decided that, despite the price, I would love to stay there one day. I saw the deer once more and encountered a red squirrel, the photograph of which is a blurred attempt to capture it though the hastily stopped car window. As ever it is not the quality of the photograph but the memory it recalls that counts.

The final destination of the trip was the Isle of Skye. Many years ago, Brian and I left the Isle of Mull after a couple of wet, cold and miserable days. We had seen little wildlife and the views had been lost in the clouds. We were disappointed. We drove through a snowstorm in Glen Shiel, which was a perilous journey that covered the car in inches of snow as the wipers fought hard to keep the windscreen clear. Eventually we took the ferry from the Kyle of Lochalsh to Kyleakin with 'Over the sea to Skye' playing on the car's cassette player; yes, it was that long ago. As we drove away from the town, we were greeted by the bluest sky we had ever seen and equally blue water. In the distance the top of the Cuillin Hills were dusted with snow. Brian pulled the car to a halt and we got out and stood side-by-side marvelling at the view. It took our breath away. We fell instantly in love with the island and had found our spiritual home.

The next day it rained constantly, and I drove from my bed and breakfast in Portree, to Uig, Duntulm and round to the Old Man of Storr, circling the top of the island. I drove on to the Sound of Sleat to the Clan Donald Centre at Armadale castle. Sadly, Covid meant the restaurant was closed but I was still able to buy lots of McDonald goodies in the gift shop. With the anniversary of Brian's death approaching, I had a list of items I wanted to collect on the trip to lay on the ground where his ashes were buried. I had already accumulated a few pebbles from places that meant something special to Brian and at the Clan Donald centre I was able to purchase a few more. Back in Portree I found a garden centre and bought heathers to plant in two large pots in my garden. I wanted to create a Scottish tribute to Brian.

It was whilst I was on Skye, as I sat in a lay-by, that I made yet another video for the SIBC. I wanted to share with them where I was and the reason for my visit. I do not know why I felt it was the right time to mention that I was a grieving widow but for some reason it was. And so, I told the world that despite all my jolly posts throughout the past few months, I was grieving the loss of my husband. I was astonished by the response I received when I posted the video on my return. Sometimes you need one person to start a conversation for others to feel they can join in or open-up about their own feelings and many SIBC members seemed to suddenly feel they could share too. They could share the loss of a loved one, a husband, a wife, a sibling or child and the Facebook group was a safe place to do so. It remains special for so many of us to this day.

The sun came out on my last day in Scotland, rewarding me with magnificent views of the Highlands as I headed to the airport and took the flight south. Back at Heathrow I collected my car and headed home. As I drove up to my house, Vix appeared from my neighbour's garden. Quickly, I got out of my car and Vix paused on the fence when I called her name. She gave a waft of her brush and then headed off across the road. The timing was almost perfect, and it was so good to know she was alive and well.

The day after I returned from Scotland was my first wedding anniversary. In my mind I relived my Wedding Day, Brian slipping the ring on my finger, and how tired he was by the end of the ceremony but also the look of love on his face when he first saw me in my wedding dress. I cried a lot. It was not the way most people celebrate their Paper Anniversary. Having made it stoically through the trip to Scotland, the floodgates opened, and I spent most of the day sobbing my heart out. Brian was gone and I was alone. Even today if you pick at that scar, you will open the wound beneath. With the passage of time, I have learned to leave alone the scars caused by the death of my parents and Brian. Reliving the darker days is too painful. As I sat in a chair feeling sorry for myself, Mew jumped up onto my lap and bumped my nose with hers. She walked around in a circle before settling down, tail tucked neatly out of the way. I could feel the warmth of her body on my legs, her gentle purring just audible. As I ran my hand over her soft fur I could feel myself calming down and I knew I was not alone. Mew seemed to know when I needed comfort. My journey through grief would have been so much harder without her.

Jem is a 'with you' cat. When she was a kitten, she would sit on my lap and enjoy a tummy rub but somewhere along the way things changed and now, although she still enjoys having her tummy rubbed, she prefers to sit near me instead of on my lap. I wonder if it is in deference to her mother. Now, if I go upstairs for too long, I hear her calling to me and I reply, "I'm up here, Jem," where upon there will be the sound of paws pounding up the stairs to join me as she mutters, "I didn't know where you were." At night Mew lies on me or beside my head and Jem curls up at my feet. Have I mentioned how much I love them? They are my family. I adore them both and that is not a word I use lightly. I have no idea how I would cope should anything ever happen to them.

Over the next few days, Vix returned each day for eggs and chicken, although the chicken had to be at the right temperature. Vix was no longer interested in chicken that came straight from the fridge. She looked healthy and the fur on her face and cheeks was fluffier. I assumed her body was getting ready for the colder days ahead and she now spent little more than ten minutes in my garden each day. It was a far cry from the afternoons when she would fall asleep for an hour or more. I missed her companionship but was pleased that she was healthy enough to be able to live a proper fox life.

As September drew to a close, I saw a young vixen on the night camera and was sure I had seen Fluffy too and Tux settled into the shelter he had decided to call home.

Above: Vix growing ever fluffier.

Above: Such a beautiful vixen.

October 2020

The Fox year-October

Many people will see foxes in the autumn as the dispersal process and the hunt for food continues.

It rained a lot at the beginning of October and Vix often arrived looking more than a little damp. She was not as hungry as she had been. I went out, clad in large rain mac and flowery wellies, to top up the fat ball feeders and put a bowl of food into the shelter for Tux so he did not have to come out into the rain for food, big softy that I am. I turned around and there was a bedraggled ball of orange fur.

"Oh, sweetie you are so wet! Why don't you go in the shelter?" I asked Vix.

Two big brown eyes looked up at me.

"I'm very wet." Vix appeared to say.
"You certainly are. How about some chompy-chicken?"
Vix ate several pieces including two on the bone. Lots of satisfied bone crunching took place and Vix took a drumstick away for a midnight snack. I went back indoors to dry off.

Above: Vix, looking fit and healthy.

I was beginning to think I was channelling a fox as, the following day, I had just cut up her chicken when I looked outside and there was Vix sitting in the garden all dry and fluffy despite the recent rain. Vix enjoyed one egg, cracked into her bowl, and I thought she wanted another, but Miss Fussy Fox was not sure what she wanted but chompy-chicken went down well. At dusk Tux and Hunter had a bit of a growling match so I used my teacher's voice to separate them and turned around to discover a certain fox sitting in her place in the dark. We had a chat about the traffic on the roads and the nights drawing in as Vix munched her way through the evening menu. She had another couple of bone crunching pieces of chicken before heading off on her rounds.

I was glad I had seen other foxes on the SIBC because I was beginning to wonder if I was feeding Vix too much and she was getting fat, or as I called it 'looking very solid', but it appeared to be the normal process to bulk up as the year entered its final quarter. It was a sign that Vix had a good supply of nutritious food too. I also worried that Vix was relying on me for all her food but when I looked out in the garden one day, she was burying something in the vegetable patch, foxy feet busily scratching at the soil. I had yet to feed her so whatever she was burying had not come from me. It was reassuring to know Vix was perfectly capable of taking care of herself.

Vix's visits continued to be unpredictable. One day I was teaching and there she was at 2.20pm. On another day she did not make her first appearance until after 5pm. When she arrived as I was teaching on Skype, I dashed outside to give her something to eat and returned to my teaching as Vix departed over the fence. And then she was back and looking in the window, giving me her squinty smile and wondering if I was going to come out again. Of course I did, I could never resist being with her, even if it was for the briefest of moments. She meant the world to me and had given me a new outlook on life.

Above: Vix squints a 'hello'.

After teaching I went back out into the garden to do some digging. It was always good to go outside and take some exercise after a long period of screen time. I was still clearing up as dusk fell and there Vix was yet again. We chatted and all was right with the world. Although I would video many of her visits and post them on the SIBC Facebook page there were also times when I did not turn the camera on and just enjoyed being with Vix, talking gently to her and allowing her to simply be. I loved our time together when there was no rush, no timetable to fulfil and no reason for her to dash off.

Having sorted through my husband's vast tool collection I was determined they should be passed on to someone who would use them and not simply be melted down for scrap or thrown in a landfill site. Throughout the house clearance process, I was determined to throw away as few of his possessions as possible. I had already taken numerous bags to an Animal Rescue charity shop and a hospice shop. I had taken car loads of 'stuff' to the local recycling centre, carefully sorting metals and cardboard to place them in the correct receptacle. And finally, there was a trip to the section for small electrical appliances.

Brian and his Dad had loved to work on their various car and motorcycle engines and in the house there were boxes of tools that he had bought for himself or inherited from his father. I have never seen so many spanners, screwdrivers, and socket sets. I was determined that these would not simply go into metal recycling and found, after an internet search, WorkAid. WorkAid take tools, sewing machines and other unwanted appliances and send them overseas for use in centres training people to develop a trade. They may also be used to make up toolboxes for people starting out on their own. Strangely, on the way to his house, on the day I was driving the two hundred mile round trip to WorkAid, Brian's car alerted me that it had low tyre pressure. I pulled into a garage to inflate the tyres correctly. It was almost as if Geoff, the car, knew it would have a load to carry later and thought it best to have his tyres inflated at a garage rather than on the hard shoulder of the motorway. When I reached Brian's house, I loaded up the car and drove to the home of WorkAid. I was pleased that my carload of goodies was well received. Brian would love to know that his tools will once more be held in a grease-covered hand, helping someone to get another car started and I would not be surprised to learn he had a hand in the car alerting me to his low tyre pressure too. Brian would always keep an eye on me and the car I drove.

Vix came by as dusk fell and it had started raining. Despite being tired from the long day of driving I went outside to offer chompy-chicken. I foolishly sat down on the garden bench to be with her and found out too late just how absorbent my trousers were. There is nothing like a wet bum to remind you to think before you sit down. Vix enjoyed the chicken but, somehow, I knew from our fox/human chemistry, that she wanted an egg in its shell to take away. I placed an egg on the ground and she picked it up carefully between her teeth before heading on her way.

A few days later, knowing I would not be there when Vix came by, I left a couple of eggs out for her. I am glad to say she found them but according to my neighbour she spent some time still looking for me. My heart swelled to know that a wild fox was searching for me, perhaps wanting my company, even though she had enough food. As much as I would always like to be there, I knew it was good for Vix to know there were days she would have to rely on her cache of food. It had worked well during my trip to Scotland and would hopefully do so again.

Above: Fluffier and fluffier.

I was out potting up some winter pansies, hoping to add some colour during the winter months, when Vix visited. She came three times in a day which was unusual. At dusk, as I sat crossed legged on the decking, Vix came closer still. I received a few wet nose bumps so perhaps Vix was still wondering what I felt like. I would have loved to have been able to lay my hand on her back to feel her. Part of me regrets never reaching out a hand to feel that fur for just a moment but the sensible side of me knows that would have been wrong.

Above: What's so funny?

I had more work to do in the garden and when my brother was finally able to visit, he helped pull the overgrown iris' out of the pond, the process of succession being well underway. The plants had reduced the pond to half its original depth. We had to cut through the iris' thick root system to divide them and salvage what we could. Many of the other plants had been strangled by the roots. I replanted a few and left the rest around the pond in the hope that any trapped animals would be able to make their way back into the water. The plants were given a thorough sniffing by the cats, but Vix did not appear at all bothered. It was wonderful to see my brother and it was acceptable for him to visit me as he was part of my 'support bubble'. If you lived alone, as I now did, you were allowed to join with another household, but only one other household, for company, support and the benefit to your mental welfare. I asked Vix if she would like to join my bubble, she made no comment, but I decided to add her to my bubble anyway.

In mid-October, a new fox appeared. From the shape of its head, it looked like a young male and I wondered if this was Vix's, now grown-up cub, Fluffy. Either way I was delighted to see him. If it was Fluffy, and I convinced myself that it was, it meant he was healthy and doing fine on his own and that he could still find his way to my garden. He was certainly a handsome chap.

Above: Is this Fluffy?

Thursday 22nd October is my nan's birthday and even though my maternal grandmother died in 1971 I still think about her a lot. She had a huge influence on my early life and so it was nice that on her birthday, Vix decided to spend some time sitting close to me. It would be nice to think it was because she had missed me. Chicken was chomped and Vix enjoyed the cut-up chicken skin but once again I had a 'feeling' she wanted to take away an egg. Sure enough, when I placed one on the ground, Vix picked it up and was off over the garden fence. The road sounded terribly busy and I literally held my breath listening to the cars and praying not to hear the screech of brakes. I did not hear anything to worry me. For now, at least, she was still safe.

With the darker days and October looming, my mood plummeted. My birthday was approaching, and I was faced with 'celebrating' it alone. I have always tried to make birthdays special for others. I would buy a cake, cards and select presents I hoped would bring the person joy. I worked extra hard to make my parents' and Brian's birthdays special. I even buy Mew and Jem a card and a present on their birthday. With a birthday carrying such significance for me the idea of being alone, on my special day, depressed me. I faced the reality of buying a cake, lighting my own candles and singing 'Happy Birthday' to myself and this time it would not be just when washing my hands. It was a sad prospect. Added to that in less than a month it would be the first anniversary of my husband's death. I would be by myself on that day too and the sense of loneliness was becoming overwhelming. Every task grew bigger; every morning getting out of bed became an effort.

I recognise the symptoms of depression in myself. I become weepier and less tolerant. Insignificant things irritate me and I spout "for fuck's sake" more than is healthy or appropriate. I do not usually swear but when depression resurfaces it is a telling sign. I lose interest in things and everyday tasks become a burden. Having spent a good part of one particular day crying I took myself out to a local woodland and chose a different route through the trees, treading a path I had not travelled before. The colours of the sun through the autumn leaves were beautiful as were the trees reflected in the lake, but even the beauty of nature could not help. They reminded me too much of the day the previous year when a nurse from a local hospice came to sit with my bedridden husband so that I could have a moment of respite. I went for a drive and took photographs of the glorious colours of the autumn trees and now I am reminded of what followed every time I drive past them. I still feel guilty at leaving him for a few hours. It hurts my heart. From now on I fear autumn is going to be a difficult time.

I may have Post Traumatic Stress Disorder or at least some element of it. It is only now that I can release the feelings of horror I experienced as I watched nurses fill the one I love with chemicals in the hope of killing the cancer growing inside him; as I watched him cry out in pain as he tried to turn in bed, and as I tried to keep him positive when we both knew he was going to die. Although he never wanted to have 'that' conversation, we both knew. When they took him into hospital for the last time and they told me 'he could die tonight' as they covered him in a blanket filled with warm air, I put on another brave face. His blood pressure was so low he could not keep himself warm. Even then as he told me 'I'm not going anywhere', I had to be positive for him before stepping out of the cubicle and sobbing my heart out as I sat on a small plastic chair. All around me were doctors and nurses tending to other patients or glued, as they always seem to be, to their computer screens. I chatted to a young woman suffering from Sickle Cell Anaemia and we did our best to comfort each other, each turning to a stranger for support in a time of crisis. At the time I could not let my own fears, and desire to scream, surface. I did my crying away from my husband because I did not want to worry him. Now the horror returned, and then deep body-wracking sobs were released. After a good cry I would either pick myself up and find a task to keep me busy or have a good sleep. Sometimes I slept in the armchair for hours, often with Mew snuggled on my lap. It was a deep sleep of mental exhaustion, the sort where you wake with a crick in your neck and a mild feeling of rejuvenation. I could face the next day after all and then a red fox would stop by.

I think Vix had a stopwatch stuffed somewhere in her fur, sort of like the White Rabbit in Alice in Wonderland. She came by three times one day, each time almost exactly one hour after the previous visit. I assumed she had a route she followed, that led her back to me an hour later. Some foxes have circular paths they repeatedly tread, and I assumed it was the same for my friend. I wished I could attach a tiny camera to her to see what she did and where she went. There is never a wildlife cameraman around to set up a Fox-Cam when you need one. I did not realise Vix was there when I entered the garden, then I looked up and saw her sitting, like ET in the cupboard amongst the toys, amongst the blue flowerpots by the pond. She gave me a look as if to say, "Hello, just waiting for you."

Above: I looked out and there she was, waiting..

Vix had become fussy about what she ate but from her bulk she was clearly not hungry. Although chompy-chicken was not always desired, Vix loved to have an egg 'to-go'. Sometimes I would not see her until after dark and I would go out to offer her an egg and receive a nose-bump. Sometimes I would receive a text from my neighbour informing me that she had seen Vix and given her a pouch of cat food. Vix was a very well-cared for fox and despite all I was going through she continued to make me smile.

My birthday grew ever closer and my heart was heavy. Brian would have made it special, arrived with flowers and a present or two. We would go out to our favourite restaurant for a meal, and I would have a glass of wine and get squiffy. All that changed when the cancer was diagnosed. Last year it had been a huge effort for Brian to climb out of bed and walk downstairs to join my brother and I for a piece of birthday cake and three weeks later he was gone. This year, I was all alone. I was worried that it would be too much to bear. That I would spend the day crying and knew I had to do something to prevent that, but what? I could go out, but where? And with whom? Whatever I did it would remind me that the person I really wanted to be with was no longer there and that I was alone. And so, I invited the Self Isolating Bird Club to join me for a virtual party to celebrate my birthday. I focused on the virtual party by making Rice Crispies in chocolate just like my Mum used to make for me and of course I topped them with a Smartie. I bought myself a small cake and a bottle of wine. My brother and friends were going to speak to me via WhatsApp I told myself it would be all right. The anticipation of an event is often worse than the event itself and I had been increasingly emotional as the day approached; it loomed like a dark cloud over everything I did.

I had no idea that the SIBC would be there to save me. When I logged onto the computer on my birthday and went to the Facebook page there was message, after message, after message from the SIBC members. Marian Pierce, a fellow Foxy Lady, and now very good friend, had sent me a video message and her kind words made me cry. There was even a post from Chris Packham and Megan McCubbin and a photograph of them holding up a sign saying 'Happy Birthday Marion'. It was beyond words. I burst into tears at the kindness of so many people, none of whom I had ever met. Between them they had turned a day I was dreading into one I will never forget; one filled with so much love, so much thoughtfulness and kindness that I am still overwhelmed by it. I had to say thank you.

SIBC posts Thursday 29th October 2020

I cannot thank you enough SIBC.

I am writing this through a veil of tears but happy ones.

I am not the sort of person people do things for, it's usually me doing things for them so I am overwhelmed by your kind words, artwork and love.

Then to see Chris and Megan sending me a Birthday message was just beyond words. 🐼🖤

I cannot comment on all the posts at the moment as Facebook thinks I am a bot or spammer if I reply to too many but I will gradually get to you all.

I will have to hug each and every one of you when the SIBC murmeration happens, so get there early!

My last post today unless Vix comes by. (I fear she has forgotten to get me a gift and is off hunting last minute rats or mice at the local BP garage 😖 *)*

Many of you have no doubt heard enough of Marion Veal and her birthday by now, but here is a cake and a cuppa to share with me. I made chocolate rice crispies as a tribute to those my Mum used to make me as a child.

Thank you all once again for making me feel so very special. You are all amazing xxx

It was such a special thing the SIBC members did.

Vix reappeared the following day. Maybe she had decided to allow me the limelight on my birthday. I spotted her on the other side of the road and went and sat in the back garden to wait for her, but she did not turn up, so I went out to the front of the house to see if she was there...we must have passed each other because she emerged from between the houses carrying an egg in her mouth. I called her name and she stopped, looked at me a bit confused as to why I was there, before going on her foxy way. However, she kept stopping and looking back at me. I was worried I would distract her from crossing the road so went indoors. Soft wombat that I am, I was happy to know she was all right.

We do not 'do' Halloween in the United Kingdom, in the same way they celebrate in the United States. Having visited California in October I have seen houses bedecked with spiders' webs, skeletons, ghosts, fake blood and gore. Even Disneyland and Universal Studios turn themselves 'Halloween'. With the coronavirus still on the loose there were no tiny witches or vampires at my door this year. However, there was a certain young lady in a fox outfit. Vix turned up around 5pm, her costume was beautiful, her tail bushy. She was not interested in chompy-chicken which continued to be a surprise but she did want an egg. It was strange how now that it was darker, she was coming in the dark and wanted less food. I thought she would have arrived earlier.

It might have been a Saturday and Halloween, potentially a happy time of the week, but the news was full of rumours of another national lockdown in England. The local lockdowns and the three-tier system that had been in place for a while, appeared not to have produced the reduction in the 'r' rate (reproduction rate of the virus) the UK Government hoped for. The number of people dying from Covid-19 was expected to exceed all predictions. In an unprecedented move the Prime Minister Boris Johnson addressed the nation in a Saturday evening Press conference. He was joined by the Government Chief Scientific Advisors. Intensive care beds were filling up again and we could run out of acute treatment beds in just a few weeks if we did not go back into lockdown. Doctors and Nurses could be asked to choose who would live and who would die. We were at crisis point and our hopes for an early end to the pandemic were dashed. We had to do what was for the benefit of all. We had to save lives.

Thursday 5th November 2020, Bonfire Night in the United Kingdom, would be a very different affair from the usual family gatherings and organised firework displays. Once again, we had to stay at home or work from home if we could. Non-essential services would close. Pubs, bars, restaurants would close and only be able to offer a take-away service. Schools and Universities would stay open. There was a great deal of discussion as to whether it was the right thing to do. The Government's priority was to keep children in education. I was lucky as this meant my own job would continue albeit with new restrictions. Single person households were once again allowed to form a 'bubble' with another household. People over 60 were told to protect themselves. The furlough system, where the Government paid a proportion of employees' salaries whilst they could not work, was extend until December. Once more, the mantra was Stay at Home, Protect the NHS and Save Lives.

I could feel the sense of fear and confusion as people were interviewed on television and the tone of the Government briefings expressed the real fear of the number of people who may die. It was a scary time. Hopes had been dashed. There was a sense of foreboding. We had coped during the first lockdown as spring turned to summer and the days grew lighter and we could sit outside. In the dark days of November, it would be very different, very isolating. Something compelled me to make a video and post it on the SIBC Facebook page. It was my way of trying to reassure everyone that if we followed the rules things would be okay. We had to stay positive. Look how they had helped me on my birthday. I was amazed at the number responses and how well it was received. Something as simple as a message from a fellow sufferer could reassure people living on their own or with no one to turn to for advice, that this would end one day, we just had to remain strong.

November 2020

The Fox year- November

The vixen may already be looking for a den in preparation for giving birth to the cubs she has yet to conceive. Some vixens prepare two or three earths in case their den is disturbed, and they must move their litter.

After the announcement by the Prime Minister, that England would enter another national lockdown, 1st November 2020 dawned the same as any other Sunday. I had a lie in, despite the usual attempts by Mew and Jem to make me get up and give them food. Taps on my nose with a paw, walking over me, swishing my face with a tail, did nothing to rouse me from my bed. Eventually two cats snuggled in beside me to wait it out. I did not spring out of bed on a Sunday, not that I spring any day. Sunday means a slow start, a snuggly dressing gown and a cup of tea as I catch up on emails and Facebook posts.

Later in the day Vix appeared and, well-trained, I dashed out into the garden as soon as I saw her. I cracked an egg into her bowl, and she lapped a little then stood back.

Did she want chicken?

No, thank you.

Was it an egg? An unopened one?

Yes, please.

I placed an egg on the ground.

Vix looked at me, carefully picked up the egg and was away over the fence.

About thirty minutes later she was back and took a second whole egg I had left out in the bowl. Fifteen minutes later she was back again and peering in through the window at me. Out I went once more. Maybe I should fit a revolving door?

Surely you don't want another egg 'to go'?

Yes, please.

What are you doing with them all?

Vix refused to say but the egg was carefully carried away and I had the feeling that somewhere she was building up a large cache.

The following day I had a fabulous day-out at the British Wildlife Centre on a photography day. It had been booked well before the latest lockdown announcement and occurred just before the new one began. All safety precautions and social distancing guidelines were adhered to as we went from enclosure to enclosure meeting the animals up close and had the opportunity to take wonderful photographs. There were only three of us on the 'course' but that meant more opportunity to get the photographs we wanted. I was happy to have the chance to take some nice photographs but equally excited to get closer to the red squirrels, wild cats, and foxes. Our guide for the day was able to answer all our questions and impart interesting information about the animals we saw. Meeting the gaze of a wild cat kitten and the golden afternoon light on a tawny owl were something to behold. But I was often conflicted. Should I be enjoying myself when I was grieving? Then I would ask myself what Brian would want, and he would tell me not to be silly. He knew how much animals meant to me, how soft I was about them and he would want me to have a good time. I told his photograph all about the day when I got home. I am sure he would have approved.

I could not keep up with my foxy friend. I was in the garden in my flowery wellies and armed with secateurs, clipping branches off shrubs, when there she was on top of the shedlette. We frightened the life out of each other, neither expecting to see anyone. We gave each other a look and took a moment to get our breath back. I made my way down the garden to the bench and sat down. Once I was back in my seat, and thus where she expected to find me, all was well. The chompy-chicken I kept in a box in the fridge was a bit whiffy, so I did not give her that. I am sure it would have been fine for Vix, after all how long does a piece of cached chicken fester in the ground? However, I never wanted to give her anything that might make her ill. Fortunately, an egg was deemed adequate. Somewhere out there, there was a huge pile of eggshells or a giant pile of raw eggs. I had the vision of someone uncovering them and thinking a turtle had hauled itself miles inland to lay them.

I left the trail camera on that night to see if Vix came back later and unfortunately two rats turned up instead. I knew I had one rat (and we all know you never have just one rat) living in the compost bins. I had seen him/her out during the day. I do not mind rats. I have looked after many and know them to be clean, intelligent creatures. My worry was that neighbours would see them too and put down poison and I did not want that making its way through the food chain to the cats or foxes. Ratty was able to climb the pear tree and get to the birds' fat balls. Then she (I was convinced it was a she) enjoyed a relaxing swing in the tray underneath as she twitched her little whiskers. I had watched her pop out of the compost heap, scurry along the fence and poop in the bird food tray. I made the decision to stop feeding the birds for a while and to not leave any uneaten food out. I tried sprinkling peppermint oil around the rat runs and the compost heaps, letting the compost in the bins get wet in the rain and blocking the holes under the fence. Time would tell if that was enough to encourage the rats to move on. I was not hopeful.

On Thursday 5th November 2020, Lockdown 2 began. I suppose the UK Government chose the fifth of November as the start of the second lockdown to prevent crowds gathering at firework displays. A wise decision but I felt sorry for all the families who had been looking forward to a fun evening out and for the vendors and organisers who once again would lose income. The pandemic would see many people suffer financially and many businesses close before any form of normality returned. However, for the local wildlife it was a bonus. Every year the explosions and deep booms of fireworks frightens thousands of domestic and wild animals across the country. Dogs cower, cats cannot settle, and horses are disturbed in their stables. What Vix and her fellow foxes would think of the sudden flashes of light and cracks and bangs, I could not tell but on past Firework Nights it has sounded like a war zone. That evening fireworks were still set off in neighbourhood back gardens but a few less than in a normal year.

I was out in the garden, on the first day of the new lockdown, sprinkling chilli pepper about, as you do. One of the rats had been out in the garden earlier blatantly chomping on something in broad daylight so I felt a bit of persuasion to move on was in order. I had received lots of advice from the members of the SIBC about rats and sprinkling crushed up chilli pepper near their runs was one of them. The peppermint oil had not worked but I was happy to try another natural method of persuasion. It avoided the need for poison, so I was willing to give it a go.

As I was talking to Hunter and Tux about performing their cat duties, and encouraging the rats to move on, they decided to have a full-on fight. I hope it was not over which of them was supposed to be doing the rat scaring. Teeth, claws, scratching, and biting ensued and quite literally, fur flew. Language was used that you would not want a kitten or your grandmother to hear. I gathered it was more to do with who had the right to be in my garden than about the rats. The answer was, of course, both of them, but since he had taken up residence in one of the cat shelters, Tux clearly felt the garden belonged to him.

When they eventually broke apart, after a lot of arm flapping and shouting from me, along with a dousing of water from a quickly grabbed watering can, I looked them over. Hunter was fine but subdued. Tux had blood dripping from his face and ear. Everywhere he walked he left blood spots on the ground. I had no idea how badly he was hurt but knew I had to do something. I telephoned my vet. If I could get him into a carrier would they be able to see him? Yes. I grabbed Mew's cat carrier, placed it in the garden and threw in a handful of cat treats. Never having been trapped in a carrier before, Tux wandered inside, his desire to fill his stomach winning over any pain he felt from his wounds. I closed the door swiftly behind him. Got him! A puzzled Tux found himself suddenly riding in my car on his way to the vet.

Once there, I put on my face mask, telephoned to announce my arrival and waited in my car for the vet to come to me. This was the new norm when visiting the vets. I explained what had happened and they took Tux inside. Tux had to be sedated as he was 'a bit feral' and was not happy at being trapped. He was given worm treatment, steroids for his skin condition and antibiotics against infection. His wounds soon stopped bleeding, the skin around them was shaved, the wounds were then cleaned and treated. The veterinary team spotted a few older wounds and kindly treated those too. A few hours later £140 was gone from my bank account and Tux was out in the garden chomping on some Felix cat food. The things you do for a stray cat you love. My neighbour informed me that Vix came by looking for me whilst I was out with Tux and she had given our foxy friend some chicken. It had turned out to be quite a busy Bonfire Night after all. The next day Tux was quieter and avoided conflict with Hunter and Ginge, the local ginger cat. When Vix turned up I asked her not to laugh at Tux's bald spots. Who knows what she thought had happened when she saw him on her visit to collect an egg 'to go'.

Despite sprinkling chilli powder around the garden, I still had a rat problem. Having stopped putting out food for the birds I missed them desperately. The sparrows sat in the bushes tweeting at me bewildered. What had they done? Why was there no food? Over the years since I have been feeding them, the number of house sparrows that visit my garden has increased from 5 to over 50 and to see them arrive at the feeders and find them empty was heart breaking. Even Mr Robin sat and chirped forlornly at me. Who would have thought that the lack of birds in your garden could be so depressing? My mood plummeted. Every time I saw a bird arrive only to find the feeders empty, I felt like crying and on occasions I did. Along with Mew and Jem, the animals in my garden were my only companions. Their antics made me smile and they reminded me that life continued.

And then Mr Rat appeared and along with him three adorable offspring. No! Tiny rodent feet clasped the branches as they explored the bushes and the pear tree. Tiny whiskers twitched and they were adorable. Now there were five rats! Mr and Mrs Rat did their best to herd their youngsters back to the compost heap but as soon as one was brought back to the fold another would sneak off in a different direction. I was conflicted. I liked them; they were a lovely family. The baby rats were sweet with tiny hands and whiskers but...It would not be long before five rats became more rats, and someone called the council to get rid of them in an unpleasant way. I had a word with Tux about earning his keep and encouraging them to move on with a good hard stare. He asked for Dreamies cat treats instead.

As the weather became increasingly November-like, that is wet, windy, dark and damp, Vix came less often. I envisioned her snuggled up in her den making her way, slowly, through the huge pile of eggs we knew she had. I kept an eye on the garden and made sure I had food available when she did arrive. One afternoon she was sitting by the pond when she asked for an egg. I was given a nice nose bump and finger nuzzle as Vix gently took the egg. She headed off, over the fence, with it firmly in her jaws. She was back about 15 minutes later, had some cat food and then another egg. Finally, as it was just beginning to get dark, she was back again. She wanted some more cat food and it was good to see her eating food instead of just going off with it. At least I knew she had eaten and not buried it somewhere another fox might find it. I may have insulted her when I said she was looking 'solid'. I mean what woman wants to be called 'solid'. What I should have said was, she was looking well prepared for winter, but the damage had already been done. I received a look.

Vix did not appear for the next couple of nights but I spotted the young male fox, who may have been Fluffy, out in the garden. It was clearly a time of change in the fox world. Others on the SIBC were reporting changes in their fox's behaviour too. When Vix returned it was all about the eggs. As I spoke to her, I held up an egg and her small pink tongue appeared. Yes, the eggs were, definitely, the food of choice. What was wrong with chicken? Why was that no longer desirable? Were eggs easier to cache? Less likely to be stolen? Did Vix have another source of food which meant she no longer needed any I offered? Was she chomping her way through earthworms and beetles? Was the egg to store for later? I do not know the answers to any of these questions. All I knew was I enjoyed every moment of her visits however brief they had become.

The middle of November marked the first anniversary of Brian's death. As the day approached, I found myself becoming more and more emotional. The anticipation of the anniversary was hard. It brought back memories of all he suffered; the day he was rushed into surgery; the moment the doctor said, 'large tumour', 'incurable', 'palliative care'; the first day of chemotherapy; how scared we both were knowing the side effects he might suffer; seeing him curled up in bed sleeping most of the day and then, as the tumour grew bigger, witnessing the pain it caused him.

I had not seen many birds in the garden since removing the food, I was plagued by rats (overly dramatic I know but that was how I felt at the time), Tux had been hurt and dripping blood, I was still sorting through my dead husband's things, my house was a mess and I no longer saw Vix as often as I used to. After a few months people assume that, as you are not obviously distressed, you must be better, but grief comes in waves and it is something you have to suppress to get through the day and function. I was sad and melancholy. It was another 'first' to get through and proved to be an emotionally draining time. The light had gone out of my days, I could see little point in anything and I sat and stared at nothing in particular. The world held no joy or interest for me.

However, thanks to the wonderful people of the SIBC and their overwhelming love on my birthday I knew I could get through it. I just had to think outside the box and do something that would make the day special. I had a card made with my name and Brian's cut out, in a paper silhouette, on the front. Paper being the material assigned to a first wedding anniversary. When Brian died, I was advised, by grief counsellors, to write down everything I was feeling. I could not do it then. The emotions were and still are too raw. I did not want to relive the horror of it all, once was enough. For it was horrifying, watching the man you love slowly deteriorate before your eyes until he can no longer move for the pain and his heart can no longer pump blood around his body; to see him lying dead in hospital and to hold his hand until it grows cold. On the anniversary of Brian's death, I went to the cemetery and mixed some soil from Glencoe into the ground where his ashes were buried and placed on top stones from his favourite parts of Scotland. When I returned home, it all came flooding out. I took off my shoes, gave Mew and Jem a quick stroke then fell to the floor in the kitchen and sobbed my heart out. And then I wrote this poem.

Grief by Marion McDonald Veal

Grief is the sorrow, here to stay,

when a memory's sparked of a brighter day.

Grief is the crying on the kitchen floor,

for the one you love who is here no more.

Grief is the photograph hanging on the wall,

of a time and place that began it all.

Grief is the places you'll no longer go,

and the future world he will never know.

Grief is discovering the ones that care,

with hearts of gold who are always there.

Grief is the people you both knew,

no longer in touch, it was him not you.

Grief is the number you no longer call.

and the care you take not to 'delete all'.

Grief is the calendar marked with days,

that must be faced with come what mays.

Grief is the slippers under the chair,

no longer worn but always there.

Grief is the trying to find the light.

in the darkest days and the loneliest nights.

Grief is the things forced to face alone,

feigning strength when you really have none.

Grief is the clothes he'll no longer wear,

but to give away you cannot bear.

Grief is the things he will need no more,

to throw, to keep or forever store?

Grief is the memory of his toughest fight,

and the battle lost under Autumn light.

Grief is the hand that's not there to hold,

and the love he declared with a band of gold.

Grief is the tears that begin to fall,

on a plot of soil beside the wall.

Once again, the natural world was there to save me. Mew nuzzled my hand and Jem stood nearby a concerned look on her face as I cried. Brian was right, it was wonderful to have another heartbeat in the house, or in my case, two fabulous little heartbeats. I reassured them both with a fuss of their fur and a few cat treats.

I saw Vix at the front of the house having an argument with Fluffy. I recognised my 'solid' fox and her fluffy-tailed youngster. At least I knew she was well, and I discovered Tux had moved into the small shelter closest to the compost bins where the rat family lived. It might have been a coincidence, or he may have actually heard me asking him to pull his weight and realised I needed help. Either way I waited to see what happened. I went out into the garden and the robin landed on a branch near me and was still there when I returned with a handful of mealworms. And finally, as dusk fell, Vix arrived. She came close and gave my hand a nose bump leaving wet, fox, nose-moisture on my skin. I felt sure she was saying thank you for the egg. A day of tears turned to one of comfort.

Above: Vix turns up later in the day.

But things were about to change.

These posts I left on the Self Isolating Bird Club Facebook page may explain how worried I was when I no longer saw Vix regularly.

Sunday 22nd November 2020

Vix turned up at dusk and posed by the fountain, looking gorgeously fluffy and healthy. She took away an egg and returned later for another and I can now tell you that the fur on her cheek was soft. Oh my. There was a slight brush of her face against my hand. I finally felt her fur and was ecstatic.

Feeling her fur was beyond wonderful. I know there are many people who hand feed the foxes that visit regularly but it was a line I had made a conscious decision not to cross with Vix. I did not believe it was in her best interests as much as I wanted it and I wanted to connect with her so desperately, the way I did Mew and Jem but again there was that blasted 'a line in the sand' my principles had. It made that small brush of foxy cheek fur so precious.

Above: Vix looking stunning and ready for winter.

Monday 23rd November 2020

Vix arrived one hour later than yesterday so it was already dark. She made three visits, took away three eggs, and peered in the window each time to get my attention and ask me to come outside.

Above: And there she was looking in the window.

Vix looking for me was special. Making eye contact with my little friend made me smile and warmed my heart. What a wonderful healthy fox Vix was now.

Tuesday 24th November 2020

Vix visited twice and took an egg on each occasion. When Vix jumped onto the garden fence she turned and gave a backwards glance. It was exactly the same thing she did when she disappeared last time and, as she jumped down into my neighbour's garden, I pathetically called out "Don't say goodbye!"

I would like to think she was off to watch the final of The Great British Bake Off which could explain her need for all the eggs.

It is hard to explain why I felt the way I did but I had become tuned into her body language enough to know when she wanted an egg so why not recognise another emotion? I was convinced she was leaving and not coming back; convinced she was saying goodbye and it hurt. The feeling was so real and painful.

Wednesday 25th November 2020

I have not seen Vix tonight.

Thursday 26th November 2020

The egg I left outside has disappeared again and I missed whoever took it.

Friday 27th November 2020

No sign of Vix again today. I have an egg outside waiting for her and the curtains are open, so I am keeping an eye out for her. I sat outside as it got dark in the hope of seeing Vix, much to all the cats' confusion. I did not see her. I hope she is all right.

Saturday 28th November 2020

Day 4 without a sighting of Vix. I am hoping the longer nights mean she is out and about later, when there are less people around and that will explain why I'm not seeing her. I have left out two eggs and set up the trail camera. Fingers crossed we see her.

Sunday 29th November 2020

I went out for a walk yesterday evening in the dark. Just for a walk you understand, not looking in gardens and hedges or keeping an eye out for a certain fox. Nope, just an innocent walk in the dark. Like you do. I did not see a fox but a neighbour has some lovely Christmas decorations.

However, I saw a fox sniffing about out the front of my house around midnight. It looked like Vix. So I am assuming the foxes are taking advantage of the longer hours of darkness.

Also the two eggs I left out have gone. I will be reviewing the trail camera footage later.

Of course, I went looking for Vix, she was my friend, and I hated the thought that she might be lying dead in the gutter. If I had found her body, I would have carried it home and had her cremated. I had paid for the cremation of Spot, the stray cat when he was killed by a car, earlier in the year. I carried his body back across the road, talking to him all the way and arranged the cremation with the vet. I would do the same for Vix if the need arose but fortunately, I found no trace of her.

Sunday 29th November 2020 was a very different day for me. As well as searching for Vix I was on the live SIBC broadcast talking to Chris Packham and Megan McCubbin and being beamed around the world via the internet. What an odd and amazing year 2020 was proving to be. I put on a bit of make-up, just foundation and a bit of lippy, because it turned out I am a little vain after all. And then there were Chris and Megs, on the computer in my living room, saying 'Hello' and discussing Vix and the upcoming broadcast as we prepared to go live. Fabian

Harrison was beavering away in the background twiddling all the appropriate knobs, muting, unmuting, going to video and Cate Croker was monitoring it all. It was nice to finally meet the full team as I had met Cate and Fabian via Skype in the run up to the big day. Chris, Megan and I chatted about Vix and I retold her story for those who were new to the SIBC. Vix has changed my life in so many wonderful and unexpected ways. Friends who saw the broadcast were pleased for me, others amazed and excited that I had kept it all secret. At least I had done until now.

Monday 30th November 2020

It is now 6 days since I last saw Vix. I have seen other foxes and one that may or may not have been her but clearly something has changed. I have kept the curtains open and at 9pm a young male fox took the two eggs I had left out. It may have been Fluffy. Vix has definitely not been in my garden today. Whatever is going on out there I just hope she is all right. I am beginning to think I may not see her now until the new year. It was January when I first noticed her so maybe she will go to ground for a while. I wish she could at least send a text to let me know she was all right.

Vix had become such a huge part of my life, helping me through my grief and providing an alternative focus. She helped me to look towards a new future. Now that she no longer visited me, I was feeling bereft once more. Her visits had slowly become less frequent and more erratic so perhaps that had been her way of preparing me and making the parting easier but it was also heart-breaking.

December 2020

The Fox year- December

The sound of foxes barking, and that bone chilling scream of mating may be heard in the evening and early hours of the morning as their nocturnal vocalisation reaches its peak. The dominant male and female may have paired up and be seen together. Foxes will defend their territories as the mating season draws near.

Tuesday 1st December 2020

When Vix last jumped onto the garden fence I did not know then that she would not turn up the next day, or any of the following days. I knew foxes were moving around in their territories and females may well be preparing for the mating season but, when December began, I knew I had to look for Vix. If she was dead I had to know. As in many things in life it was the not knowing that proved so difficult to cope with. I knew she could survive on her own, knew she had other sources of food. She had disappeared for days before and returned, often a little the worst for wear but at least she was alive. I put on my boots and jacket and headed out of the house. As I walked along the road, I scoured the kerb and gutter for any sign of a fox or its remains. A piece of fur, a trace of blood, I prepared myself for it all. Fortunately, I saw none. I entered the fields where I was sure she lived and wandered along the hedgerow. I found a few trails of crushed grass which I assumed were the fox paths. Despite there being a few dog walkers and mothers with children in the distance, as I walked along peering into the undergrowth I called out, "Vix. It's Marion. I just want to know you are all right." Obviously, there was no reply. I reached into my pocket and withdrew a raw egg. I rubbed it over my wrists in the hope that it would add some of my scent to the shell then placed it on the ground under a bush. A few paces later I did the same with a second egg. When I got to the end of the hedgerow I gave one last long look back and walked home.

And then something magical happened.

That evening as I was watching television, Vix turned up in the garden. I dashed outside, grabbing some food as I went. She backed away slightly, watching, as grinning foolishly, I lowered myself to sit on the ground. I held out a piece of chicken and an egg. I told her how worried I had been and that I had gone looking for her. She came forward and gave my hand a nose bump. My heart swelled as she left her fox nose-moisture on my skin once more. She sniffed the chicken but did not want it. Then she came forward and picked up the egg I had placed on the ground. I think she only took it out of politeness. It was as if she was letting me know she was okay. Had she heard me calling her name and it reminded her of me? When she left, making that familiar jump up onto the fence, she paused, looked back at me for a long moment, our eyes met, and I knew she was saying goodbye. "Don't go," I whispered but she dropped down out of sight. I sobbed with relief that I had seen her, and she was well, but that look troubled me. I sat outside for another hour, but she did not come back, but, in my heart I felt certain she was letting me know 'all is well'.

Above: I miss this beautiful girl so much.

Afterward

As I write this in 2021, I have not seen Vix since that day.

I do not know if I will ever see Vix again. Will she have more cubs and bring them to see me? I would like that. When she left she was fit and healthy. Did that mean she was able to claim the prime fox territory? Was Fluffy born in the only space she could find but now she is able to stand up for herself and claim a more preferential den site? Whatever she does or wherever she goes I console myself with the thought that she was in excellent condition to cope with all life throws at her. I miss her so much and she will always have a special place in my heart, Vix has changed my life and I will forever be grateful to my fox friend.

With my newfound confidence, at the end of 2020, I produced a calendar of photographs of Vix which members of the SIBC kindly purchased and it raised £500 for the South Essex Wildlife Hospital. I also have a range of T shirts, sweatshirts and tote bags featuring Vix on a Teemill site. I am using the profits from the sales to make donations to the South Essex Wildlife Hospital, The Fox Project and The Fox Man. Vix's legacy has spread far and wide as I work to pay it forward.

With the encouragement of the Self Isolating Bird Club I wrote a children's book about Vix. Kathryn Coyle, who I met through the SIBC brought Vix to life through her amazing illustrations and the book, Vix the Lockdown Fox was published by Stour Valley Publishing in 2021.

There are new foxes in my garden. Since I last saw Vix I have met Little Fox, Brushetta, grown up Fluffy (who I originally called Big Dog), Cubby, Stick and Limpet. I love watching them and I will champion our urban foxes at every opportunity.

One thing I have learned over the past few years is that there are no guarantees. We must live each day as it comes. That does not mean we should not hope for the future but my attitude to life has changed since the death of my parents and my husband.

At the start of 2020 Vix and I were both wounded and in need of love and care, we gave it to each other with mutual trust and helped each other heal. Vix helped me through an emotional year and to deal with my grief, which I am still trying to do. She led me to the Self Isolating Bird Club and the incredible kindness of strangers. Vix opened a whole new world for me, led me to new friends and, from the messages I received, she has clearly helped others too. I hope I will see my fox friend again one day. I keep my ears open for the clatter of the fence.

Author Bio

Marion has always loved writing. As a child she scribbled stories about Lassie and Daktari, as an adult she wrote about her favourite cowboys, but it was the arrival into her garden of a fox she called, Vix that led to the publication of her first book, a children's story titled Vix the Lockdown Fox and illustrated by Kathryn Coyle.

Marion is a science teacher and her love of the natural world has seen her travel in search of whales, bears and other amazing wildlife.

She shares her home with her beloved cats Mew and Jem and her garden with the birds, bees and foxes.

References:

South Essex Wildlife Hospital

https://southessexwildlife.org/

The Fox Project

http://foxproject.org.uk/fox-facts/sarcoptic-mange/

The Fox Man

www.facebook.com/thefoxmanuk/

The National Fox Welfare Society

http://www.nfws.org.uk/mange/Mange_FAQ.html#Whatcausesm
ange

Vets All Natural

https://vetsallnatural.com.au/digesting-bones-gastric-acidity-
salmonella-dogs-cats/

The National Fox Welfare Society

Year Of The Fox (national-fox-welfare.com)

Organisations

Workaid - Tools for Life – The Queen's Award for Voluntary Service

Workaid.org

British Wildlife Centre

britishwildlifecentre.co.uk

The Hawk Conservancy Trust

www.hawk-conservancy.org

Follow Marion's adventures on her website: marionveal.com

Vix T-Shirts, Sweatshirts and Tote bags available at:

https://vix-the-lockdown-fox.teemill.com

Shop Vix Portrait, the Alphabet Collection, Watercolour and more.

Profits from teemill sales continue to support:

The South Essex Wildlife Hospital,

The Fox Project

The Fox Man

Printed in Great Britain
by Amazon

72495484R00180